FORTUNE
COOKIE
DEVOTIONS

MICHELLE
TAYLOR

Get
WR TE
PUBLISHING

Book design by TLCGraphics, *www.TLCGraphics.com*
Cover: Tamara Dever, Interior: Erin Stark

Edited by Lisa Ann Johnson

First Printing: May 2017
Get Write Publishing
ISBN: 978-1-945456-82-4

*This book is dedicated to those that believe
there has to be more to life.*

TABLE OF CONTENTS

Acknowledgments ix

How to Use This Book xi

It Takes Everything 1
- Surrender Your Burdens 3
- Stop Praying the Process 7
- Surrender Produces Fruit 11
- Giving 15
- Submission 19
- Weekend Challenge 23

**It is Better to Deal with
Problems Before They Arise** 29
- Procrastination 31
- Armor of God 35
- Salvation 39
- Read Your Manual 43
- Preparation 47
- Weekend Challenge 51

**A Good Laugh and a Good Cry,
Both Cleanse the Mind** 57
- Smile 59

- Passion 63
- Seasons 67
- Empathy 71
- Meeting Together 75
- Weekend Challenge 79

Life is a Play. It's Not its Length, but its Performance That Counts 85

- Premature Loss 87
- Practice What You Preach 91
- Agape Love, Pt. 1 95
- Agape Love, Pt. 2 99
- Salt and Light 103
- Weekend Challenge 107

Life to You is a Dashing and Bold Adventure 113

- Adventure in Surrender 115
- Dying to Self 119
- Alive in Christ 123
- Obedience 127
- Christian Walk 131
- Weekend Challenge 135

You Will Succeed in Whatever Calling You Adopt 141

- Spiritual Gifts 143
- Joy and Peace 147
- Puzzle Pieces 151
- Out of the Box 155
- Comfy with the Uncomfortable 159
- Weekend Challenge 163

A Great Pleasure in Life is Doing
What Others Say You Can't 169
- Great Faith 171
- Following Christ 175
- Discipline 179
- Joy Unspeakable 183
- Leadership 187
- Weekend Challenge 191

Don't Let the Past and Useless
Details Choke Your Existence 195
- Forgiveness 197
- Discernment 201
- Time to Move 205
- Face Forward 209
- Look to the Heavens 213
- Weekend Challenge 217

You Cannot Love Life Until You
Live the Life You Love 223
- Created 225
- Be You 229
- Live 233
- Intentional 237
- Fullness of Joy 241
- Weekend Challenge 245

Even the Toughest of Days
Have Bright Spots, Just Do Your Best 249
- Pruning 251

- Perspectives. 255
- Countenance 259
- Focus on Christ 263
- Submit 267
- Weekend Challenge. 271

Your Next Interview Will Result in a Job 277
- Interview with God 279
- Divine Purpose. 283
- Your Calling 287
- Following 291
- Transformation 295
- Weekend Challenge. 299

**You Will Reach the Highest Possible
Point in Your Business or Profession**. 305
- Your Purpose in Christ 307
- Faith it 'Til You Make it. 311
- Persistence. 315
- Fight the Good Fight 319
- Run Your Race. 323
- Weekend Challenge. 327

Plan of Salvation 333
Resources 337

ACKNOWLEDGMENTS

I THANK GOD FOR ALL HE HAS PUT IN ME AND DONE IN ME, to me, and through me. Even though I haven't always embraced the process, I know that I could never have done it without Him and the processes that I've been through. They were definitely necessary.

Much thanks and appreciation to Rekesha Pittman who suffered through many annoyances to help me get this book published. Thank you, Lisa Ann Johnson, for making sure the contents were properly polished and suitable for consumption. Special heartfelt thanks to Tamara Dever and Erin Stark, my graphic design specialists, for taking this project from clueless to awesome in less than 90 days!

To my assistant researcher, prayer partner, and proofreader, Mona Moyer, may God bless you mightily for your service. Kudos to Linda Clark who never failed to give me honest feedback and insight every step of the way. Thank you, Pam Parker, my sister from another mother, for being pivotal in reviving me and building my confidence to do more. I just knew your graduation tied to my destiny. Thank you, thank you, thank you, Christopher and Angelica Montgomery, for taking me on. You've pushed me out of my comfort zone, stretched me past my limits, and convinced me to soar to higher heights. Without that, I probably would have never even attempted to do this.

Last, but definitely far from least, kudos to my family. My mom supported me along the way by being my sounding board and giving good advice. Most importantly, thank you to my husband Brandon and our children Danny, Andrea, Johnny, Carissa, Valerie, Eden, and Dylan for sacrificing and putting up with my crazy schedule. I know it's been a bit rough. May this book mark a turning point in our lives! I love you all more than you can ever imagine.

HOW TO USE THIS BOOK

THE BOOK YOU ARE HOLDING IS NOT YOUR TYPICAL DEVO-tional. It is as unique as the person that wrote it. It has been written to challenge you, induce thought, and provoke action. This book is meant to take you on a very real adventure with Christ.

God had me collecting the fortunes from fortune cookies for quite awhile. Other people began to save them for me too! Every time I would read one, scriptures and topics with life applications came to mind. In the beginning, I was clueless, and just being obedient. As time went on, I realized that I was supposed to write this book. Honestly, I probably have enough fortunes saved up to cover an entire year.

There are enough devotions and challenges here to keep you going for about three months if you choose to do a devotion each weekday and pick a weekend challenge to focus on. I know many devotionals tend to keep all of the devotions the same length. I chose to be different and vary the lengths a bit so you can pick and choose how much time to spend each day. Being from an era that Choose-Your-Own-Adventure books were very popular, this seemed a suitable approach for a life adventure!

Yes, this book is laid out like a traditional work week. There are five days of devotions that are all from the same fortune but based on different topics. Following those five days is a weekend challenge section. This section contains five challenges that directly correlate to one of the devotions from that week. You can choose to do one or all five. Some are more challenging or time-consuming than others. You can do everything in order or bounce around and do things according to your schedule as you see fit. You may want to do all the devotions and then all of the challenges, or mix and match. The freedom is there, and the layout is simple enough for you to do just that.

To get the most out of this book, set aside a special time and place to read it daily. This book will likely cause you to laugh and cry, so you will probably want to have a box of tissues handy. More importantly, make sure you have your favorite Bible and writing supplies such as a notebook and pen. You might even want a snack, fortune cookie, or a drink.

Some of the devotions and challenges may cause you to feel a bit convicted by the Holy Spirit, but remember that there is no condemnation in Christ. This is a good thing because the conviction can bring about much-needed change when it's allowed. There are several activities and challenges spread throughout this book. Many involve writing because there's something about writing that helps us process things and engrave them into our memory.

You may be wondering why I used so many different Bible translations. There are many reasons for my doing this. I can't emphasize enough the importance of having a Bible that you can easily understand and are comfortable with. I prefer some translations simply because of their choices on capitalization and punctuation. Others are just easier to understand because they use more common everyday language. Some translations were used because they are familiar classics that I remember from my childhood. I wanted to give you, the reader, a sampling from translations you may already be familiar with as well as some you aren't. This way you can get an idea of what's out there.

One way to look at this book is as a springboard with lots of mini springboards within it. Please remember that each prayer written in this book is simply another springboard for you. You might decide that there are some that you want to pray word for word, and others that you may want to change up a little or a lot. Make it personal and keep in mind that prayer is just a conversation between you and God.

You might notice that most of the prayers are similar and references or names of God are slightly varied. Daddy God is used in some of the prayers to encourage and increase intimacy. I know some adults that still call their earthly father "Daddy." Some may be uncomfortable with this, and that's fine. You don't have to use it if you are uncomfortable with it. Again, make the prayers in this book your own. I wanted to discuss prayer in a more discreet manner since it isn't the main focus of this book.

There is a resource list at the end of this book as well as the Plan of Salvation. These are more tools for you to use as needed. The resources listed are for you to obtain or volunteer services, and also for you to connect others to resources as well. This book should challenge, stretch, and grow you. It should stir up that fire deep down in your soul, and cause you to go deeper in your relationship with Christ. My prayer is that you will be encouraged, have increased faith to step outside of the box, and ultimately change your life!

IT

TAKES

EVERYTHING

SURRENDER YOUR BURDENS

I COULD PROBABLY WRITE AN ENTIRE BOOK BASED ON THIS fortune alone! The theme God continued to impress upon me with this one was "Submission." I can simplify it in one little phrase: "Give it all to God, and give God your all!" In this day and age of compartmentalized Christianity, that phrase may be over-simplified. I'm going to break it down for you a bit more over the course of this next week.

God wants all of us; not just bits and pieces here and there. Give it ALL to Him! Every hurt, every hang-up, every flaw, and lay it all down at Jesus' feet. He's the only one who can handle it all. You were never meant to carry all that baggage with you for your entire life! Imagine every issue you have as a full-sized piece of luggage. Now, imagine every component of each issue as a carry-on bag. Could you carry all those bags from one end of an airport to the other? Of course not! You'd need help, and that's just what the Lord wants to do for you through the power of the Holy Spirit!

Then Jesus said,

> "Come to me, all of you who are weary
> and carry heavy burdens, and I will give you rest.
> Take my yoke upon you. Let me teach you,
> because I am humble and gentle at heart,
> and you will find rest for your souls. For my yoke
> is easy to bear, and the burden I give you is light."

MATTHEW 11:28-30 NLT

Jesus didn't say, "Some of you." He didn't include a list of guidelines. He said, "Come!" This is an open and personal invitation to you!

> O my people, trust in Him at all times.
> Pour out your heart to Him, for God is our refuge.

PSALM 62:8 NLT

God is literally inviting you to unload! How great is that? You can leave ALL your luggage with Him! You don't have to carry it around another second! Re-read Matthew 11:28-30. You are being offered three things in this passage and it's up to you to receive them.

First, He is offering you to come to Him for rest. Who doesn't want rest? We all want rest and peace in our lives.

Secondly, you are being offered an exchange. You are invited to trade your load for His. We need to learn to see things through God's eyes. He will teach you, and the burden He will give you to bear will be light in comparison to what you are lugging around right now! That's not to say that your life will be all sunshine and roses, but rather that He will teach you how to handle the burden.

Lastly, God is offering you a partnership. He's not asking or expecting you to do life all on your own. You don't get brownie points if you try either. He is promising to teach you. Since He is humble and gentle at heart, He will help you carry the burdens He puts on you and find rest for your weary soul.

Trust Him and pour your heart out to Him. He's not going to make fun of you or ridicule you. You certainly won't be condemned. The Lord is NOT going to leave you. He's going to take your luggage for you!

What are the three things you are being offered?

What's your baggage? What is burdening you and weighing you down? List all of your issues. Examples: shame, guilt, self-doubt, past hurts, etc.

What are your carry-ons? List the components of each issue. Here's an example of what one of yours might look like.

SELF-DOUBT	
I've messed up before.	I'm not qualified.
I feel inadequate.	Others criticize me.
Others tell me I can't do it.	Others laugh at me when I try.

Now pour your heart out to God. You can use this prayer as a starting point, but I encourage you to make it your own and as detailed as possible. Remember, prayer is simply talking to your Best Friend Ever-God!

Heavenly Father, I am coming humbly before You to unload my burdens. I am weary and heavily burdened. I need Your rest. I hunger and thirst for Your peace and rest. I want to partner with You Lord. Help me to see things the way You do. Right now, I am releasing my issues (list them all) and all their components (list them all). I am trusting You to trade what burdens me for what burdens You. I am laying it all down at Your feet. Please, Lord, give me Your perfect peace and rest. Help me not pick these things up again. Teach me to handle the burdens You intend for me to handle and also how to leave the others alone. I love You and trust You. I ask these things in Jesus' mighty name. Amen.

STOP PRAYING
THE PROCESS

HOW MANY TIMES HAVE YOU BARGAINED WITH GOD IN prayer? "Lord, if You do this, then I'll do that." You're making God a promise that you'll likely not keep, and that puts you in a dangerous place. Let me tell you a little secret: You'll forget! You'll forget what you promised God and chances are you'll even forget what you prayed for!

Maybe you want a new house and you don't have good credit, a good job, or money for a down payment. Your prayer might look something like this:

Lord, please give me a better paying job. I really need money for a down payment on a house. Please help me clean up my credit and save money for a down payment. Help me get a new house. In Jesus' name, amen.

STOP! No, no, no!

If you've ever prayed prayers like this, and I think we all have at some point, stop right now! You are praying the process. You're telling God how to get the job done, and blocking Him from having His perfect will and way in your life.

That prayer lacks submission. What was the ultimate goal in it? You want a new house. God can do it through many ways though. He may even open a door for you that wouldn't require any money or credit. Maybe He's waiting on you to be obedient in some area of your life first. Whatever it is, His ways and plans are better than ours! Who do you think you are? Why would you want to tell God how to do His job anyway?

When we go to the Father in prayer, we have to be open and submitted. What do I mean by that? We have to go to God open to His will and way. Rarely will God answer prayers the way you think they should be answered, or the way you would do it if you did it yourself. We should rejoice and be glad about that because He always does it better!

"My thoughts are nothing like your thoughts,"
says the LORD. "And my ways are far beyond anything
you could imagine. For just as the heavens are higher
than the earth, so my ways are higher than your ways
and my thoughts higher than your thoughts.

ISAIAH 55:8-9 NLT

Sometimes it takes everything in us to give up our control. When we go to God in prayer, we must give Him complete control over the situation. We have to have faith that He can and will do the thing His way and that His way is far better than ours.

Read John 2:1-12. Go ahead; I'll wait. This is where Jesus turns water into wine. Did you notice anything in that passage? This was the first time Jesus revealed His glory, yet Mary and the disciples believed in Him. How much more should we believe in Him since we have the Bible and have seen God work in our lives as well? Notice, Mary tells them to do whatever Jesus says. They understood submission and obedience, and they applied it to their lives. Are you applying it to yours?

The next time you go to God in prayer, don't beat around the bush. Tell the Lord exactly what it is that you want. Don't worry; you won't surprise Him. He already knows, but He wants to hear it from you. Be careful not to pray the process. Pray for the end result, the actual thing you are desiring. Then, be sensitive to the Holy Spirit. Maybe God is waiting on you to do your part. Obedience is key and a large part of submission. Has God asked you to do something that you haven't done or even taken the first step towards doing? Do you have an area of sin in your life that God has been asking you to address? Sometimes an answer to a prayer is simply waiting on our obedience to the Lord. (That's not to say that this is the case with all prayers that appear unanswered.)

Do you have an unanswered prayer in which you have prayed the process? If so write it down in a new way that doesn't tell God how to do it and shows that you are trusting Him and taking your hands off. Remember the ultimate goal of your prayer, such as desiring a new house. Now, pray this new prayer.

Have you seen God work in your life? How? Are you aware of anything that God has asked you to do, but you haven't done it yet? If so, what do you need to do at this point to be obedient?

Now go to your Father in prayer. Remember that prayer is a conversation with God. Be sensitive to the Holy Spirit and what He is trying to tell you.

Father God, I come humbly before You open to Your will and Your way. Lord, I love You and want to be obedient and submissive. Please teach me to pray with faith and abandon leaving it all to You, and to also stop praying the process. Help me to hear You with clarity so that I can obey. I ask these things in Jesus' name, amen.

SURRENDER PRODUCES FRUIT

IT TAKES ALL! GOD WANTS YOUR ALL. IT'S NOT ABOUT YOU. This life is not your own. You are His! You were bought at a very high price on the cross at Calvary.

> Don't you realize that your body is the temple of the Holy Spirit, who lives in you and was given to you by God? You do not belong to yourself, for God bought you with a high price. So you must honor God with your body.
>
> **1 CORINTHIANS 6:19-20 NLT**

> My old self has been crucified with Christ. It is no longer I who live, but Christ lives in me. So I live in this earthly body by trusting in the Son of God, who loved me and gave himself for me.
>
> **GALATIANS 2:20 NLT**

And so, dear brothers and sisters, I plead
with you to give your bodies to God because of
all he has done for you. Let them be a living and
holy sacrifice-the kind he will find acceptable.
This is truly the way to worship him. Don't copy
the behavior and customs of this world,
but let God transform you into a new person
by changing the way you think. Then you will
learn to know God's will for you,
which is good and pleasing and perfect.

ROMANS 12:1-2 NLT

When you accept Christ as your Lord and Savior, you are agreeing that as much as He is yours, you are His. You agree to let Him transform you and make you new. I've heard many people share Saul to Paul stories but for most of us, the truth is, it's a slower process. The key lies in dying to one's self daily. You must remember that it's a daily process, and I think many of us forget that. It is no longer we that live, but Christ living in us! How awesome is that?

Read Romans 12:1-2 again. Did you catch that? The way we live our lives is our worship to Him! Look back over your life from right here at this moment back to the moment you accepted Christ. Have you been transformed? Has your life changed? Do you see sin or habits that you have truly repented of and turned away from? Good for you! Praise God for those. What sin or habits do you need to work on now? Go ahead and do a written assessment. List the sin/habits that the Holy Spirit has helped you conquer and those that you are now facing.

Read Galatians 5:16-26. Again, how we live our lives is our worship to Him. There should be fruit in your life. The fruits of the Spirit are Love, joy, peace, patience, kindness, goodness, faithfulness, gentleness, and self-control. List the fruits that you frequently display and those that you struggle with. Now, if you are really daring, ask a close friend which fruits of the Spirit you display. This will help you know if your list is accurate or could use a bit of adjustment.

I know today's devotion may have been a bit difficult for you. Let's take it all to God in prayer. Please feel free to add to it and make it your own.

Lord, I come to You today humble and broken. I long to live a life of acceptable worship to You. Thank You for Your patience with me and helping me conquer sin (list your sins/habits that you have conquered). I know that I am still a work in progress. Please help me to conquer the sins and habits that You would have me focus on right now. Increase the fruit of Your Holy Spirit in my life so that I can live that life of acceptable worship. I ask these things in Jesus' powerful name. Amen.

GIVING

WHAT DO YOU GIVE TO GOD? I MEAN TRULY GIVE, AND I'M NOT talking about your problems and burdens this time. God wants your all, but what do you give? Do you give of your time in serving others and, specifically, spending time with the Lord each day? Do you give your resources by regularly tithing to your church, donating items or money to worthy charities, and giving to those in need or those less fortunate than you? Do you give God credit for the good things in your life such as a raise, a new car, or improved health? Or, do you take all the credit for it because of how hard you think you worked for it?

In this day and age, we tend to take a lot of things for granted. When we truly live according to His Word, we remember that everything we have is merely on loan. We are simply stewards of the things we have in our possession currently. Are we being wise stewards of the things the Lord has entrusted to us? Today I'd like you to read the Parable of the Talents (money) in **Matthew 25:14-30**. It's OK, go ahead and read it now. This book isn't going anywhere!

The servant with only one talent did nothing with it. He basically just sat on it and was called wicked and slothful, or lazy. This parable is not only referring to our money but also our time, physical talents, spiritual gifts and anything else that God has entrusted to our care.

I don't know about you, but I don't want to be wicked or be called "wicked!" I love the Lord, but if I'm not properly utilizing all He's given me, I am being wicked and lazy. I must admit that there were times I was guilty of being lazy. Whenever I got tired, frustrated, or just plain overwhelmed at all that I needed to get done; instead of doing what I could, I would just sit around and talk about it. It's no longer a lifestyle for me, but at one point it was easy to slip back into it.

In this passage, we are clearly told that we will only be given what we can handle. If we want more, we have to do more! To those who are given much, much will be required.

> But someone who does not know,
> and then does something wrong,
> will be punished only lightly.
> When someone has been given much,
> much will be required in return;
> and when someone has been
> entrusted with much,
> even more will be required.
>
> **LUKE 12:48 NLT**

Maybe you fall on the other end of the spectrum though. Do you have "much" and handle all of your affairs tightly by managing your time, gifts, money, and talents well? If so, good for you! Do you also give God all the glory or do you keep it for yourself?

> Remember the LORD your God.
> He is the One who gives you power
> to be successful, in order to fulfill
> the covenant he confirmed
> to your ancestors with an oath.
>
> **DEUTERONOMY 8:18 NLT**

Some translations say, "power to get or produce wealth." All that you have comes from God. Yes, even your paycheck. Sure, you work hard for that paycheck, but it is your duty, and the Lord has given you the ability to do that work. We need to change our perspective on how we look at things in our life. ALL that we have is a gift from God; be it our children, spouse, cars, home, money, etc. When we don't keep things in this proper perspective, we run the risk of taking things for granted and being prideful.

No matter which end of the spectrum you fall on (or somewhere in between) there are probably areas that you have overlooked or could do better with. That doesn't make you a bad person or mean that you should beat yourself up over it. We should all strive to be and do better though, and with the help of the Holy Spirit, we can. Today, let's ask the Lord to show us where we need to improve.

Heavenly Father, I thank You and praise You for all that I have, even the things that I have worked hard for. Please help me to keep things in proper perspective and not become proud or boastful. Show me the areas of my life that I need to manage better and give me the wisdom and strength to improve those areas. Make my life a shining example for those around me. In Jesus' name, I pray, amen.

SUBMISSION

IN A SENSE, WE ARE ALL SLAVES TO SOMEONE OR SOMETHING. For some people, it may be drugs or alcohol (as in addiction). For others, it may be television, money, video games, or social media. Take an in-depth and personal look at your life. What do you spend most of your time doing? Who or what dictates or drives your life? Who or what gets the majority of your focus and attention?

Praise God, that for most of us, our Master is chosen! Unfortunately, in these times, due to financial issues, many feel enslaved to their job and boss. However, our only true Master is Christ.

This letter is from Paul,
a slave of Christ Jesus,
chosen by God to be an apostle
and set out to preach his Good News.

ROMANS 1:1 NLT

Don't you know that when you offer
yourselves to someone to obey him as slaves,
you are slaves to the one whom you obey—
whether you are slaves to sin, which leads to death,
or to obedience, which leads to righteousness?

ROMANS 6:16 NIV

What does all of this mean? Well, with the exception of those who are truly abducted and sold into slavery, we generally choose who our masters are. Yes, slavery still exists. You can learn more by contacting the resources listed under human trafficking in the resource list at the back of this book. Christians have one headmaster, and that is Christ. God puts people in our lives that we are also supposed to be submitted to, like teachers, bosses, spouses, church leaders, etc. It is the natural order of things. Without being submissive to a teacher, you won't likely learn much, and without submission to your boss, you'll probably lose your job.

Submission doesn't mean being a door mat, or simply enduring abusive relationships. The word "submission" is often seen as a negative in this day and age of independence, but it simply means, "accepting one's authority and being obedient." Most people don't go around breaking the law intentionally. True submission is done willingly and is an act of humility. This is NOT something bad!

Likewise you younger people,
submit yourselves to your elders.
Yes, all of you be submissive to one another,

and be clothed with humility,
for "God resists the proud,
But gives grace to the humble."

1 PETER 5:5 NKJV

Submission to other people is working together toward a common goal. It was never meant to be oppressive. There will be times that people will submit to you, and times that you will need to submit to others. There are times, such as in marriage, where the person you submit to also submits to you. This is part of God's plan. Nowhere in the Bible are you encouraged to live a life of complete independence doing whatever you want!

Now, back to those of you who are enslaved to your job or boss. I strongly encourage any of my readers that are in an abusive situation with their job to look for other employment. I know that this can be difficult, but trust the Lord to help you through this process. He may even put people in your path to help. Some of you may be enslaved, but you aren't in an abusive situation.

How does God want us to handle our jobs and bosses? The answer is in God's Word! Grab your Bible. I'll wait. Now read Colossians 3:22-25. It clearly tells us that slaves or servants (depending on what translation you read) are to serve as though they are serving the Lord Himself. The Lord will reward you because your Master is Christ. It takes everything. Work diligently, giving your best effort. Show up to your job on time and be properly equipped and dressed. Do your best to get along with your coworkers and work peacefully together as required. Maintain your integrity, work willingly remembering your reward, and be glad that you have a job and the ability to work.

And you shall remember the LORD your God,
for it is He who gives you power to get wealth,
that He may establish His covenant which
He swore to your fathers, as it is this day.

DEUTERONOMY 8:18 NKJV

I know that this may be a sensitive subject for many of you. I hope that it stretches and grows you in the faith and maybe even pulls at your heartstrings as you contemplate these things. Let's pray.

Father God, I come humbly before You seeking Your will and Your way. Please reveal to me things that I have allowed myself to become a slave to. Help me to be a slave to You and righteousness. Help me to work diligently and with excellence in all that I do and to remember that I am doing it for You. Lord, help me to be in proper relationships of submission and to remember what the true meaning of submission is. Please deliver those that are in ungodly slavery situations. I ask these things in Jesus' most holy name. Amen.

WEEKEND CHALLENGE

SO WHICH ONE OF THIS WEEK'S TOPICS WAS MOST DIFFICULT for you? I know it's counter-intuitive for our culture to accept a challenge, and this week may have been a bit rough for you, but I dare you to pick a challenge (or all five) and grow even more! Do you struggle to let go fully, or is your issue one of trying to control the future? Could you stand to have a little (or even better, a lot) more fruit in your life? How are you doing when it comes to giving and submission?

Let it Go

Do you have something that you just can't seem to let go of? The Christian music group Unspoken has a song called *Follow Through*. It talks about how it's easy to put something down for a moment, but sometimes the hardest thing can be not picking it back up again.

I have a daughter with complex medical issues. Hundreds if not thousands of times I thought I had given it all to God, but He was quick to show me I hadn't. It took me at least seven years! I'm not proud of that, but sometimes it's a process. This weekend why not try something that finally worked for me when nothing else had?

Choose one issue to focus on. The first morning, during your prayer time, discuss the issue with the Lord. Ask Him to provide you with godly people that can help you through this process, and to remind you whenever you begin to pick it back up again. Share your struggle with the person or people you've been given. Be accountable to them. Give them permission to remind you. The key is in learning to recognize when you begin to pick it up so you can focus and change your behaviors. Whenever you are trying to pick it back up, go into prayer and if necessary talk to one of your people.

Lose Control

What's the most important prayer that you need to be answered right now? Choose one thing that you can spend the weekend on focused in prayer. Start a prayer journal and write down today's date and the end result you are in need of. Write a prayer in that journal that is full of praise, asking for the end result that you are looking for (the thing you need), and for the end result of others as well. Does that prayer have a hands off approach? Does it allow God to answer His way?

Are you still struggling with how to formulate your prayer? Here are a few tips:

- Use your own words and keep it simple.
- Praise (thank) God.

- Say what you need or want and why. Keep it short and simple!
- State what you are requesting for others and why.

Tell Him that you are OK with it. Ask for strength, courage, and wisdom to be able to deal with it whenever He chooses to make it happen.

When your prayer has been answered, go back and write in your prayer journal, as detailed as possible, how and when your prayer was answered.

Produced to Produce

We were created to produce. We are commanded to be fruitful and multiply, to reproduce. Let's look at the fruits of the Spirit again. They are love, joy, peace, patience, kindness, goodness, faithfulness, gentleness, and self-control. They are all different, yet similar and from the same source.

In the natural, a fruit salad tree (and its fruit) is a good example. A stone fruit tree is a type of fruit salad tree. This tree produces peaches, apricots, nectarines, plums, and peachcots, some even having different color varieties. All of these fruits come from the same tree, but they are each different yet similar. I love the way God gives us things in the natural to help explain the spiritual (even if these trees are multi-grafted).

These fruits are so closely intertwined that they can be hard to flesh out. When the fruits of the Spirit are in action in your life every day, you begin to develop tangible fruit in your life that others can see. People will be drawn to you, and seek your company and advice. When you put that fruit to work, you draw others to Christ.

What's one way you can put your fruit to work this weekend? Could you volunteer at a food pantry or shelter? Do you have an elderly or shut-in neighbor? You could sit with them and listen patiently to their stories. Do you know a single mom? Can you give her a break and love on her kids this weekend, maybe take them to the park or a movie and just spend the weekend getting to know them better? Exercise those fruits so they can grow!

Give to Live

Frequently when we give it helps another to live. Sometimes, what we give can seem so insignificant to us that we lose sight of its true value. All the while, the person on the receiving end is super grateful, seeing Christ through you and it means the world to them. Sometimes it is a literal life and death situation such as donating blood, time counseling, or a meal to someone with no means to get food. Other times when we give it actually helps us to live. Have you ever given and it 's had such an impact on the recipient that your heart just swells with joy because God used you?

Are you a packrat to any degree? I must admit that I am, however, it has allowed me to be able to meet the needs of others. Your challenge for this weekend is to evaluate what more you can give beyond your tithes, first fruits, and offerings. Do you have things just sitting around that you no longer use? Maybe you're like me and have baby clothes, and toys stashed away. Just take some time to go through them, wash them, and donate those that are still good to your local pregnancy center. This is just one example. What do you have sitting around unused or that you have an excess of? Seek a neighbor, friend, someone in your church family, or a worthy non-profit to donate these items to. Remember that you are blessed to be a blessing!

Swallow Your Pride

Submission is a voluntary and intentional action. It requires humility to allow someone else to be in charge of a project or certain set of circumstances. It requires us to swallow our pride, and allow other people to lead. Is submission particularly difficult for you?

This weekend prayerfully choose one of the people that God wants you to submit to. Maybe that person is your spouse, parent, or boss. Spend the weekend focusing on the reciprocal and relational aspects of submission to one another. That means mutual, humble cooperation and loving acknowledgment of each other's value. Realize that submission is working together with a common goal or purpose instead of always demanding your own way. Pray specifically for this person, your relationship, and your common goals or purpose. Think of some ways that you might acknowledge their value in your current relationship.

It is
Better to

DEAL

WITH

PROBLEMS

Before
They Arise

PROCRASTINATION

HOW WE DEAL WITH PROBLEMS SAYS A LOT ABOUT US AS A person. It tends to reveal our level of faith, strengths, and weaknesses. Our preparedness for certain problems can reveal a lot to us as well as others.

We can't foresee every potential problem or issue, but there are some we can. For instance, if you have a project due by a certain date and you wait until the last minute to do it, you can pretty much count on being stressed out and running into problems. This could have been prevented if you didn't procrastinate and had just simply worked on the project a little each day.

There are ways that we can prepare ourselves for unexpected problems as well. We must stay connected to our Source through prayer, praise, and worship. We need to continually wear the full armor of God, and seek Him and His will for our lives. It is when we practice these things that our reactions to problems are likely to be more Christ-like even though they may be unexpected and intense. Constantly practicing these things is how we can be obedient and prepared at all times.

Preach the Word; be prepared in season
and out of season; correct, rebuke,
and encourage-with great patience
and careful instruction.

2 TIMOTHY 4:2 NIV

First, let's deal with the issue of procrastination since it is probably the most common cause of preventable problems. I must admit that I am a recovering procrastinator. I think most people tend to procrastinate when it's something they don't like or don't want to do. Then, for some, it goes much deeper.

Some people tend to put off everything. This tends to happen when a person is depressed or battling a spirit of laziness. I think we've all either been or known a person with each of these issues.

Read Joshua 18:3-6. The tribes were apparently procrastinating, or Joshua wouldn't have addressed it the way he did. The land was theirs. They just needed to evaluate it and divide it up fairly. Joshua was going to cast lots in the presence of God, so it wasn't like they had to worry about fights amongst themselves over who got what land.

Nobody knows for sure why they were putting it off. It could be that they were overwhelmed by the size of the task, or maybe it seemed too difficult or boring. Perhaps, fear of success or change even played a part.

Fear is another co-factor of procrastination. Fear is often misunderstood. We automatically tend to think that all fear is bad. Fear in proper context has kept people safe or motivated them to do something that they needed to do, such as in a natural disaster. Other times we don't even know what we're afraid of! Fear in and of itself isn't bad. It's what we do with that fear or what we allow fear to do to us that can be bad.

We can all have a tendency to put things off, but some of us can be rather habitual about it. Do you frequently find yourself putting things off or wishing that you had done them sooner? Do you see any particular patterns? Pray, and ask God for help in this area.

Dear Heavenly Father, I come humbly before You asking Your forgiveness for the times I've failed to do things in a timely manner or fallen into the bad habit of putting things off until the last minute. Please reveal to me any patterns or unknown causes for my procrastinating. Lord, I ask that You give me strength and strategies to overcome this issue in my life. Move me to follow through with the strategies and ideas You give me. I ask this in Jesus' mighty name. Amen.

ARMOR OF GOD

AS I'VE STATED BEFORE, CONTINUALLY WEARING THE FULL armor of God is a way to be prepared for problems. A soldier in the army wouldn't dare step foot onto the battlefield without all of his appropriate gear on. Why on earth would we?

Read Ephesians 6:10-18. There are many good books and resources written on the armor of God, so this will just be a practical overview. Why are we told to put on all of God's armor? It's so that we can stand firm against the devil! Let's take a real quick look at each piece of the armor.

The first piece that we are instructed to put on is the belt of truth. The meaning of this piece is twofold. We should be living a life of integrity, and others should know that we are honest. The deeper meaning is knowing the truth though. We need to know what we believe and why. We do this through regular Bible study and continued learning.

The breastplate of righteousness is important in that it protects our heart. Satan loves to attack our emotions and use them against us. When we are wearing the breastplate, we believe in the righteousness of Jesus. We acknowledge that He is our righteousness. We know He will protect us from evil because our faith is in Him.

Standing firm is a bit easier when our feet are prepared with the Gospel of peace. What does that mean though? It means that we have a firm foundation in Christ and know the Gospel. We know it well enough that we can bring others to Christ. As Christians, we have peace in knowing that God has everything under His control.

For whatsoever is born of God
overcometh the world:
and this is the victory that
overcometh the world, even our faith.

1 JOHN 5:4 KJV

The shield of faith is what squelches the fiery darts of the enemy. It is our faith in Christ, all He is, has done, and will do that we draw on when we face difficult circumstances. We must conscientiously choose to walk by faith and not by sight.

Be sure to wear the helmet of salvation. We have the assurance that our salvation is secure in Jesus. It is how we block the negative thoughts from the enemy. We need to keep our focus on the proper things.

For the rest, brethren, whatever is true,
whatever is worthy of reverence, and is honorable
and seemly, whatever is just, whatever is pure,
whatever is lovely and lovable, whatever is kind

and winsome and gracious,
if there is anything worthy of praise,
think on and weigh and take account
of these things (fix your minds on them).

PHILIPPIANS 4:8 AMP

Lastly, we have the sword of the Spirit. It is the only piece that is used for offense in a battle. It is intended to defeat the enemy and save lives. The sword of the Spirit is the Word of God. When Jesus was tempted, His answer was the Word. We too are supposed to use the Word to defeat Satan's attacks and to save lives by bringing others to Christ.

I encourage you to take the time to study the full armor of God in more detail. You won't be disappointed. It will be well worth your time and effort, but in the meantime, be sure to wear it daily.

Lord, as I put on the belt of truth, help me to remember Your truths, to walk in them daily, and not turn away from them. Jesus, please protect my heart with Your righteousness. Pour into it to overflowing that I may pour into others. Help me to be prepared at all times with Your gospel of peace and to share it with those that I come into contact with. Strengthen me in my faith that I may constantly walk by faith and not by sight. Increase my faith. Help me to remember that my salvation is secure in You and to remember to focus on those things that You would have me to focus on. Thank You for the armor and the sword of the Spirit. Please help me to wield the sword with pinpoint accuracy. I ask for these things in the mighty name of Jesus. Amen.

SALVATION

No one knows about that day or hour,
not even the angels in heaven,
nor the Son, but only the Father.

MATTHEW 24:36 NIV

THIS VERSE IS ABOUT CHRIST'S RETURN. NOBODY KNOWS
when He's coming back. The same is true for our death,
we don't know when we'll die, but we best be prepared.

Therefore keep watch,
because you do not know the day or hour.

MATTHEW 25:13 NIV

So you also must be ready,
because the Son of Man will come
at an hour when you do not expect him.

MATTHEW 24:44 NIV

This is a command to be ready for a problem before
it arises! The issue of your salvation could be a big
problem if you've never addressed it. We won't be

given a second chance to repent, turn from our evil ways, and accept Jesus. Upon your death or the return of Christ (whichever comes first), it's a done deal. Will you be going to heaven or hell?

> Therefore, my dear friends,
> as you have always obeyed—
> not only in my presence,
> but now much more in my absence—
> continue to work out your salvation
> with fear and trembling.

PHILIPPIANS 2:12 NIV

My guess would be that since you are reading this book, you've probably already accepted Jesus as your Lord and Savior. You are probably familiar with the plan of salvation. It's always good to review it from time to time though, and if you aren't familiar with it, I've placed it in the back of this book for you. Sometimes we need to go back and re-evaluate where we stand and rededicate our life to Christ.

Take some time to read Revelation 3:14-22. Go ahead; I'll wait. This passage is dealing with the heart attitude of the people of the church in Laodicea. Unfortunately, I believe this is a very real problem in most of the churches in the US today. Have you grown lukewarm, or is your heart still on fire for Him? Maybe you've grown discouraged or apathetic. Have you gotten distracted by life?

This isn't God's will or plan for you. He has so much more in store for you! There's still hope!

"Look! I stand at the door and knock.
If you hear my voice and open the door,
I will come in, and we will share
a meal together as friends.

REVELATION 3:20 NLT

Dear brother or sister in Christ, if you are reading this book, then you are at the very least lukewarm. You probably don't need to worry about being cold You may already be on fire for the Lord, but if you're not, I'm praying that the fire inside of you be stirred up into an all-consuming fire! I pray that your fire will be so strong that everyone around you sees it. Now is the time to stir it up. Stir it up! You don't know the day or hour of the end of this life. Don't wait!

I hope that you now long to be fiery. Are you wondering how to do that? God wants an intimate relationship with you. Open up your heart the way you would do with a best friend. Let Him in. Talk to Him. No more walls or barriers. Tell the Lord everything. Sure, He already knows it all, but He wants to hear it from you.

It starts with prayer (conversation), praise, and worship. Tell God how thankful you are for all He is and has done for you. Let the Lord know the things you value and acknowledge Him. Don't leave anything out! Take your time. Reveal all and ask for His forgiveness, not only for your sins but also for growing lukewarm if you have. Pray!

Oh, Heavenly Father, stir up the fire in my heart. Make my soul long and burn for You forever. Let Your thoughts be ever present in my mind so that Your love and works flow through me and out of me. Take me to a new place of intimacy with You. Increase my fire and desire. I'm inviting You in. Please mold me and make me into all that You would have me to be. Remove anything that is not of You. Purify and cleanse my heart, oh God. Pour into me to overflowing Lord. Less of me and more of You. Have Your way in me and through me. I pray this in Jesus' name. Amen.

READ YOUR MANUAL

READ EPHESIANS 4:17-32. THE BOOK OF EPHESIANS IS WHAT Paul wrote to the church in Ephesus to strengthen, encourage, and instruct them in proper living as Christians. You may have heard it said before that the Bible is life's instruction manual, and it truly is. No, it's not going to tell you what decision to make in every circumstance, but if you really read it, you will know how to make godly decisions when it counts. Some decisions are about choice and preference while others are more serious requiring prayer and direction. The more you read your Bible and spend time with the Lord the better you'll be able to discern the two. You'll probably start making better decisions in general.

You may have questions about things in life. Believe it or not, the Bible can even answer questions. I can't emphasize enough the importance of having a good Bible. It should be easy for you to read and understand. After all, who wants to read something they can't comprehend? When you easily understand what you are reading, you are better able to focus on the content and context. That, in turn, makes it easier for you to apply what you learn in the Bible to your everyday life.

Yes, the better study, topical, and life application Bibles are not cheap, but that should tell you something. They are valuable, and technically worth more than you could spend. I encourage you to invest in yourself and your Christian walk by investing in one of these instruction manuals as soon as you possibly can unless you already have one. I know that it may mean saving the change in the couch cushions for a few months or skipping your daily fancy coffee habit for awhile, but in the long run, it is so worth it. Once you have one of these books, spend some time with it to really get to know it and all the features.

Be careful, that when you are choosing your new Bible to have plenty of time and not to be rushed. Check out the various aides that are in different Bibles such as dictionaries, maps, concordances, explanations, etc. Choose a translation and style that is a fit for you. Take the time to actually open each one that you look at and read a little bit. Compare your options. With the internet, you can probably do some or even all of your research online and even purchase one. There are many brick and mortar stores as well as online stores that sell new and used books if finances are a major issue for you.

Physical training is good,
but training for godliness is much better,
promising benefits in this life and in the life to come.

1 TIMOTHY 4:8 NLT

No, this verse isn't telling you that you don't have to exercise anymore. Nice try! What it is telling us is that physical fitness is important, but that spiritual fitness is even more important. For instance, if you spend an hour at the gym, you should spend at least that much time if not more in the Bible. Did you just say how or with what time? Don't feel bad. I used to ask the same thing until I developed a habit of getting up an hour earlier each day.

Depending on your workout routine, you can read while you work out. Treadmills and stationary bikes even have a place to set a book so you can do just that. You might even find that you can do planks longer and a bit easier while reading your Bible. Try it! You should be focused on what you're reading, and you'll forget how long you were holding that plank. You can also get an app that reads the Bible to you, though this shouldn't be abused! You still need to read some for yourself.

Some other ideas to fit reading your Bible into your day include starting your day earlier like I do or maybe staying up later. You could have lunch or coffee with the Lord and read during your lunch or coffee breaks. Maximize your time! You could listen to the Bible on your commute to and from work, but don't abuse this option by thinking that you don't have to crack open your physical Bible. Do you have small children? Read your Bible or a children's Bible to them. Watch them start to ask for more.

Do you regularly read your Bible?

How can you fit Bible time into your day, or increase that time?

_____

Dear Heavenly Father, I do want to utilize my instruction manual for life. I thank You for Your Word. It is my manual and so much more. Please show me how I can get more time in Your Word. Give me divine strategies to make it work. Help me to enjoy the time I spend, understand what I read, and learn to apply it to my life. Create a hunger in me for more of You and Your Word in my life. I ask this in the name of Jesus. Amen.

_____

Watch, if you were serious about this prayer, you will see results. It is a process, but I encourage you, to then share that process with others.

PREPARATION

Preach the Word of God. Be prepared,
whether the time is favorable or not.
Patiently correct, rebuke, and encourage
your people with good teaching.

2 TIMOTHY 4:2 NLT

THIS VERSE IS SO RICH AND HAS SO MANY POINTS. I'M GOING
to break it down for you the way the Holy Spirit broke
it down for me because on the surface it may be hard
to see how this verse relates so well to this fortune.

Be prepared, whether the time is favorable or not.
I'm so grateful to my mother for raising me with the
mindset to be prepared for anything. However, some
may think I've taken it to the extreme. I tend to over
pack when I travel, but then when someone wants
that obscure thing I usually have it for them to use!

I challenge you to develop more of a mindset like
that. It's not just about that though. What does
"whether the time is favorable or not" mean? It means
that the timing of a thing may not be convenient. I was
once driving on my way to work and came upon an

accident. I knew that if I stopped, I would be late to work. I saw that there was no one on the scene, no traffic on the country road, and a woman sitting in the damaged vehicle with smoke pouring out. Yes, I stopped and helped her out of the car, called 911, and waited with her until help arrived. I was late to work, but God covered me, and I didn't get into any trouble.

That example may be a bit extreme. What about some everyday examples? The King James Version states that we are to be instant in and out of season. Are you instant? When someone tells you they need prayer, do you pray with them right then and there, or do you have the typical response and tell them you'll pray for them and possibly even forget?

Imagine you're in a packed grocery store line and an exhausted mother with a screaming infant is in line behind you. Do you show her Christ's love and let her go before you, or do you have the typical response to just stand there silent, or even worse, stand there complaining? Do you allow God to inconvenience you? That is ultimately the bottom line. Are you available to be used by God? Are you willing to be inconvenienced?

Ah, how about correction? Few people like to be corrected, and even fewer can take constructive criticism. Then there's the other side of correction. When you have to correct someone, are you doing it in love? There is no condemnation in Christ. Therefore, when we correct someone we should not be condemning, but rather, helpful, loving, and encouraging change. How do you handle correction, both giving and receiving it?

Do you encourage people? Even your life can be encouraging to others. People that you may not even realize are watching how you live and handle everyday obstacles and situations. You might be surprised to know that there may even be people that you don't know that look up to you.

Sometimes even the simplest of things can be an encouragement to someone such as a hug, smile, or compliment. Try to give at least one compliment today. Want a bigger challenge? Compliment a stranger today. This practice will teach you to look for the good in a person, even if at first you are only noticing the external. Watch how a person's face lights up when you compliment them on something.

Don't stop with today though! Try to increase the number of people and compliments each day. You will likely find your mindset changing. You'll start doing it on a regular basis and become less judgmental. Even better, the people around you will notice and be drawn to you. Look at people through the eyes of Christ instead of the critical eyes of the world.

Heavenly Father, help me to see things through Your eyes, and to be discerning but not judgmental. Help me to accept and learn from correction and to give correction in a loving manner that is acceptable to You. I want to be ready and obedient at all times even when it's not convenient or easy for me. I know that with You I can rise to the challenge and do it. I trust You for this. You alone are almighty and all powerful, and so I ask these things in Jesus' name. Amen.

WEEKEND CHALLENGE

HOW ARE YOU DOING WHEN IT COMES TO DEALING WITH problems? Do you feel spiritually prepared for problems as they arise? Are you struggling with procrastination or getting enough time to read your Bible? Read on for this week's challenges.

Take a Step

The number one way to beat procrastination is to take that first step in something you have to do. Do you have something you are currently procrastinating about? Sometimes it's just because we are overwhelmed at the size of the task or just don't know where to start. Spend your weekend focusing and working on completing that task.

Logic often tells us to start at the beginning, but not every project has a clear beginning. For things that have no clear beginning, sometimes you can even start at the end and work your way back. Evaluate the task at hand. Determine the necessary steps you need to take and if there's a required order to them.

When there is no particular order, you've been given the power and responsibility to create order. Take that job you've been putting off. Does it have a set order? Some people prefer to do the most difficult tasks first to get them out of the way. Others prefer to work smallest to largest and build up momentum. Still, others like to mix it up or work in order of priority.

Break that project into manageable tasks. Determine the order in which you should go. Take the first step and follow through. Decide in your heart and mind that no excuse can or will stop you! Stop talking or complaining about it and just do it!

Wear That Armor

Have you strengthened your core today with God's truth? Spend some extra time with the Lord today examining each piece of the armor as you visualize yourself putting them on. Perhaps even go through the physical motions of putting them on.

Are you prepared to stand firm? Temptation comes in many forms. We must stand firm against the attacks of the enemy and do what is right, even if we think it won't matter or that nobody will know. Part of having a godly character is doing the right thing even when no one is watching!

When you are wearing the full armor of God, you can share the Gospel with greater ease. Not everyone is an evangelist, and I understand that. However, we are all called to share the gospel. Your challenge this weekend is to share with at least one person. It may simply be talking with a friend over coffee about something you've learned while reading this book, or even better, the Bible. You may even be blessed enough to lead a total stranger to Christ if you allow yourself to be inconvenienced. Wherever you are, start there and stretch yourself beyond your comfort zone. Allow God to use you knowing that you are fully covered with your armor.

Get Right with God

Wherefore, my beloved,
as ye have always obeyed,
not as in my presence only,
but now much more in my absence,
work out your own salvation
with fear and trembling.

PHILIPPIANS 2:12 KJV

What was Paul saying here? Fear and trembling in this verse does not mean that a person is supposed to be terrified of God. It tells us that we should respect and show reverence for Him. Paul was emphasizing to the Philippians that since he was not there to watch over them, that they had to be responsible for their walk with Christ. They needed to be focused on God and their Christian walk. Paul wasn't there to lead, correct, or guide them.

Read Philippians, chapter 2. How are you doing? Are you in right standing with God? Do you have good fruit? Are you on fire for the Lord?

You might not have given your life to Christ and fully surrendered. Perhaps you have, but you're backslidden. This weekend get right with God. Read the Plan of Salvation at the end of this book, and if necessary pray that prayer. Confess your sins to God and start your next week fresh with Him.

Know Your Manual

How well do you know your manual, the Bible? When Satan comes to attack, he often uses God's Word, but He twists it. He will throw enough truth in there that if you don't know the Word, you can easily be tripped up and deceived.

You must spend more time reading your Bible. I can hear some of you reading whining right now, "Where am I going to find the time to do that?" I'm glad you asked! Chances are that those of you whining the loudest are those that barely read it. That's why I've told you up front to bring your Bible, notepad, and a pen. That's why in this book, you won't find me just spoon feeding you scripture, but making you go look it up for yourself to read it. You've got to go after it yourself. Nobody can do it for you. You're going to have to work with me!

For those of you that don't spend time alone with the Lord each and every day I challenge you to start. Don't procrastinate. Do you want a better life? Then you have to be willing to change some things. Start by getting up 15-30 minutes earlier each day. Open your time in prayer and ask the Lord to show you what it is that He wants you to know and focus on today. Do this for all of next week. The following week add five minutes and do that for a week. Continue adding each week until you've doubled your time.

By the end of the month, you should find yourself more eager to spend this time with the Lord. You should be hungry for more. It should be becoming a necessary habit for you. I know you can do this!

Be on the Lookout

Part of being prepared is always looking for opportunities for God to use you. Are you ready and willing to be inconvenienced this weekend? I dare you to spend the entire weekend looking for opportunities to serve others. Be open to the Holy Spirit's leading.

It may not look the way you think it should. Your service may be something as simple as cleaning your neighbor's yard. The Lord may prompt you to go a bit further and visit someone in the hospital. You may be led to go even further to stop and pray with a total stranger. Allow yourself to be stretched outside of your comfort zone. It's OK. There's a bigger, more exciting, and better life outside the confines of your own comfort!

Whatever you do this weekend, don't stay within the four walls of a building or the walls of comfort in your own mind. Stretch yourself. Get uncomfortable and allow God to use you in mighty ways.

A Good Laugh
and a
Good Cry,

BOTH

CLEANSE

THE MIND

SMILE

A merry heart maketh a cheerful countenance;
but by sorrow of the heart the spirit is broken.

PROVERBS 15:13 KJV

ONE OF THE FIRST THINGS THE LORD BROUGHT TO MIND
with this fortune was countenance and Proverbs
15:13, along with emotions. I'm a pretty serious person, and a long time ago people thought I was sad or
angry because I never smiled. When I learned of this,
it made me sad, angry, and even a bit confused. I was-
n't either of these things. I just always had a straight
face. I was crushed when I learned my children
thought the same things about me.

In some cultures, you may hear mothers tell their
children or church mothers telling people, "You better fix your face!" This expression was most often
said to someone when they were upset, angry, or
clearly showing displeasure in their face at what was
deemed a socially unacceptable time. A good example would be a child pouting at a birthday party

because they were told they couldn't have a present because it's not their birthday.

I went through a season where God was telling me to fix my face! I had to learn the value of a smile. The Merriam-Webster website defines a smile this way, "n: to make a smile: to make the corners of your mouth turn up in an expression that shows happiness, amusement, pleasure, affection, etc. to show or express (something such as approval, encouragement, etc.) by a smile, transitive verb 1: to affect with or by smiling."

You see, by not smiling, my children were questioning my love and approval of them. It didn't matter if my heart was smiling or not. I didn't know the value and purpose of a smile, and people often thought that I was mad at them or didn't like them.

The Lord started working on my countenance, or by definition, the appearance of my face. I had to fix my face! I learned that I didn't reveal any emotions because I had grown numb and apathetic in my walk with Him. I had no idea how important and powerful a smile could be.

In this era, where the focus is on technology and social media instead of direct relationships, people are often in a hurry and don't smile at one another or greet each other. That makes a smile now of even more importance and value. Isn't it wonderful that the Lord helped me fix my face all those years ago?

Look back at the transitive verb definition for the word "smile." I believe that we as Christians are supposed to affect others with our smile. After all, they will know we are Christ followers by our love.

SMILE

Your love for one another will prove
to the world that you are my disciples.

JOHN 13:35 NLT

Smiles and emotions can be controversial, but when handled appropriately they can be very powerful, valuable, and even influential. We'll spend more time evaluating these this week.

Our joy in the Lord should be reason enough to smile, and if we look at things through His eyes, then there are plenty of things to smile about. I also learned that a smile is sharing. When we smile, we are opening up to those around us and sharing our emotions. I had a wall around me that I hadn't even realized. I didn't let many people in to any degree. Do you let people in, or do you have a wall up too?

Our smiles are frequently encouraging too. What happens when a baby learns to walk, and they see someone smile at them? They get excited. What does a smile do for you? Who can you smile at today? Be an encourager and share of yourself. Smile at someone today!

Lord, please increase my joy in You. Help me to be open to others and smile more. Allow me to see things through Your eyes and delight in the things that delight You. When I am tempted to allow my emotions or aspects of my day to spill over to someone else, please remind me to be kind and smile at someone with Your love instead. I want more of Your joy Jesus. Please help me. Amen.

PASSION

HAVE YOU EVER WATCHED THE 2004 FILM, "THE PASSION OF the Christ"? Yes, I know, it's a rather graphic movie. I think it's the very graphic nature of this film that brought so many believers to tears though. It makes us stop and reflect upon the sacrifice that was made just for us.

Communion has never been the same for me since I watched that movie. I am often moved to tears as I contemplate what Jesus went through for little ole, undeserving me. How can I not be? He suffered so greatly for me! Salvation came at the highest possible price, and I'm not the one that paid it.

I believe that this is a soul and mind cleansing cry that everyone should have from time to time. Yes, it can be painful. For me, a good cry often leads to a headache and stuffy sinuses, but it could never begin to even come close to the pain Jesus endured on my behalf.

SO THEN Pilate took Jesus and scourged
(flogged, whipped) Him. And the soldiers,
having twisted together a crown of thorns, put it on
His head, and threw a purple cloak around Him.

JOHN 19:1-2 AMP

Carrying the cross by himself, he went to the place
called Place of the Skull (in Hebrew, Golgotha).
There they nailed him to the cross.
Two others were crucified with him,
one on either side, with Jesus between them.

JOHN 19:17-18 NLT

When was the last time you thought about? I mean really thought about what your salvation cost? What do you see when you think about and read about the crucifixion? Go back and read the scriptures above and try to picture it in your mind. It's OK to let the tears flow. I encourage you to allow them. I'm not judging you, and despite what society says, tears are not a sign of weakness. In this case, they are a sign that the cost paid for your salvation and that your salvation, itself, actually means something to you.

Today, I am intentionally cutting this a bit short. I want to allow you time to deeply focus on Jesus' sacrifice for you. Allow it to truly sink in, and reflect upon it. Worship Him, and thank Him for what He's done for you.

Father God, I can't possibly thank You enough for sacrificing Your only Son, but I thank You. I value all that You have done for me through the work of Your Son Jesus. Father forgive me. I am sorry for _____ (fill in the blank) and all of my sins of omission and commission. Please forgive me for any times that I take Your work on the cross for granted. Lord, I thank You and praise You in Jesus' most holy name. Amen.

Please, make this prayer your own and add to it as you see fit.

SEASONS

PURIM IS A JEWISH HOLIDAY BASED ON THE EVENTS IN THE book of Esther. The Jewish people celebrate their deliverance from Haman's evil plot to eliminate all of the Jews in one day. They do traditional readings of the book of Esther, and whenever Haman's name is mentioned, they make a bunch of noise and stomp their feet to blot out his name.

A good laugh and a good cry refer to seasons. Ecclesiastes 3 was, in part, turned into a song written by Pete Seger and made popular by The Byrds. **Take some time to read Ecclesiastes 3:1-8.** Go ahead; I'll wait!

> For if you remain silent at this time,
> relief and deliverance for the Jews
> will rise up from another place, but you
> and your father's family will perish.
> And who knows but that you have come
> to royal position for such a time as this?"
>
> **ESTHER 4:14 NIV**

The word "time" could easily be replaced with "season." In this particular verse in Esther, Mordecai is telling his cousin, Esther, that this is her calling, season, or purpose. We were all created on purpose, with a purpose, and for a purpose. You are not an accident!

There is indeed a time for everything, and we all experience seasons. Farmers understand seasons and their importance very well. There are seasons of lack and seasons of abundance; a season to plant or sow and a season to reap the harvest. A farmer knows their job in the various seasons and does it well. A farmer won't plant when it's not the right season.

There are some seasons mentioned in Ecclesiastes 3 that some of us will never experience. On the other hand, seasons such as birth, death, weeping, laughing, mourning, joy, a time to be silent and a time to speak are experienced by everyone. These seasons and experiences are what makes us who we are. They mold and shape us; equip and train us.

It's easy for us as humans to get mad at God for the season we're in or one we went through. We have to be careful to give it to God and allow Him to use it. If we aren't careful, it would be easy to become bitter and resentful. This helps no one.

Do you know what season you are in right now? Do you know the season of those closest to you? Many times we go through seasons together such as the death of a loved one, but at other times, we are alone with God; for instance, a new job. It's good to recognize the season that you're in and that of those around you. This keeps you from doing things out of season.

Knowing the season you are in helps you to act accordingly. You wouldn't wear a winter coat on a hot summer day. Likewise, when you are in a season of lack, you shouldn't buy a brand new car. Some seasons in our life will be repeated and others won't. Often these times make us stronger and build our endurance. Hopefully, we learned from the last go around, and we will handle it better the next time. When you find yourself repeating a season, compare it to the last time you went through something similar. What can you improve or change compared to the last time you experienced this? Is there something specific that you need to change or improve upon?

Do you know your purpose and what God has placed inside of you? Make a list of your strengths and weaknesses, natural talents, spiritual gifts, and interests. What things do you do best or enjoy? What irritates you? All of these things can help you in discovering your purpose. (For further help with this you can contact GLAD Mission, listed in the resource section in the back of the book).

Mordecai saw the season Esther was in and helped her to recognize and act upon it. She had favor with the king, the people, and God. It was time for her to stand for her people. Her time (or season) to speak had come and had she not, her people could have perished.

It is my hope that you have a better understanding of seasons and their importance. I pray that you know your purpose or that you have at least started the journey towards discovering it. Let's pray.

Dear Heavenly Father, please help me to recognize my seasons and those of others. Speak to me about my purpose and how You would have me to fulfill it. Allow me to see what You have deposited in me, and give me the understanding necessary to use these things for Your glory and for the purpose that You have created me for. I ask these things in Jesus' almighty name. Amen.

EMPATHY

So that there should be no division in the body,
but that its parts should have equal concern
for each other. If one part suffers, every part
suffers with it; if one part is honored, every part
rejoices with it. Now you are the body of Christ,
and each one of you is a part of it.

1 CORINTHIANS 12:25-27 NIV

I THINK THIS VERSE IS PRETTY CLEAR. WE ARE TO HAVE CON-
cern for one another. I'm a very empathetic person by
nature, but I know that not everyone is. The Lord made
it very plain that I needed to write about empathy with
this fortune. As part of the human experience, we will
all have periods of joy and sorrow, but that doesn't
mean that we are supposed to go through them alone.
This section of scripture made that pretty clear too. We
are all part of the body.

How might the world be different and better if each
person actually showed empathy, even if only half the
time? We are living in an era of ME, ME, ME! I think

a lot of people have forgotten what empathy actually is, or worse, they've never been taught. You may be asking, "Exactly, what is empathy anyway?" I'm glad you asked! Empathy means to share someone else's feelings and experiences as if they are yours. In other words, to put yourself in another person's shoes, and be able to understand their viewpoint and where they are coming from.

> Suppose a brother or sister is
> without clothes and daily food.
> If one of you says to him, "Go, I wish you well;
> keep warm and well fed," but does nothing about
> his physical needs, what good is it?
> In the same way, faith by itself,
> if it is not accompanied by action, is dead.

JAMES 2:15-17 NIV

I have experienced this while serving in homeless ministry. A common misconception toward the homeless is that they've done this to themselves, or are addicts, alcoholics, or too lazy to work. For some this may be true, but definitely, not for all. It's not for us to judge. I've met plenty of homeless people that lost a job, were disabled, their spouse died, etc.

The path to homelessness is just as different as the person. They do have some things in common though. Most of them don't want to be homeless and never would have expected it. They are all human, they all get cold and hungry, and most appreciate any help they can get. The biggest thing to remember is that they are human beings just like you. This may sound simple, but when we remember that people are human like us and that we could just as easily be in their position, it is much easier to empathize.

Do nothing out of selfish ambition or vain conceit,
but in humility consider others better than yourselves.
Each of you should look not only to your own interests,
but also to the interests of others.

PHILIPPIANS 2:3-4 NIV

When was the last time you were able to put yourself in someone else's shoes? Do you consider the interests of others? Faith without works is dead. We don't have to sacrifice our physical life on a cross like Jesus did for us, but we should be willing to sacrifice something from time to time, if not more frequently.

Empathy goes hand in hand with compassion and respect. Each one relies and builds upon another. To have empathy for a person, you must first respect them as being made in the image of God. If you can't see a person as a fellow human being created in the image of God regardless of race or circumstance, then you'll never be able to show empathy or compassion for that person.

Genuine empathy works to move a person to an act of compassion such as hugging a person that's crying or feeding someone that's hungry. Do you really think Jesus fed the 5,000 or performed any of the other miracles without respect, empathy, and compassion for the person/people involved?

Jesus never treated them as less than or unworthy. We need to be careful to do the same.

Which area can you best improve? Respect, empathy, or compassion? For today's prayer, I want you to choose one of the following people groups:

- homeless
- persecuted Christians
- prisoners

Put yourself in their shoes. What are their needs, feelings, or wants? Create your own prayer based on this information and pray specifically for the people group you have chosen.

MEETING TOGETHER

GO BACK AND REREAD 1 CORINTHIANS 12:25-27. WE ARE THE body of Christ, and there is to be no division among us. We are supposed to work together and look out for one another. We are to be connected just as a body is connected. A lone finger can't do anything unless it is attached to a hand and working in conjunction with other fingers and the thumb. Even something you might do with only one finger you must move the other fingers out of its way, still working together!

And let us consider how we may spur
one another on toward love and good deeds.
Let us not give up meeting together,
as some are in the habit of doing,
but let us encourage one another—and all the
more as you see the Day approaching.

HEBREWS 10:24-25 NIV

I don't know about you, but I can surely use all the help and encouragement I can get! Meeting with other Christians helps us in more ways than we probably even realize. It gives us the opportunity to learn, grow, and increase our faith. When we are connected to others and meet with them regularly, we can be and receive encouragement, love, guidance, and accountability.

What is meant by "meeting together?" Meeting together can happen through regular Bible studies, church services, and even working together on projects or preparing for services. I remember a frustrating time while attending a practice for a Christmas service. Everyone was grumbling about having to leave their home in the cold when everyone already knew their parts. They were missing something deeper, the value of gathering. Some eventually got the deeper purpose once they realized some of the needs and struggles in the group that surfaced through prayer requests. Great prayer, comfort, encouragement, and strengthening came about because of that meeting.

Never miss an opportunity to meet a need or have a need met by passing up or complaining about a meeting. The reason why so many of us complain about not seeing the Holy Spirit working is that we aren't looking! We are too inward focused. We miss opportunities to see God working in us, through us, and around us because we are too busy complaining. How on earth can we ever expect anything if we aren't willing to get outside of ourselves?

In meeting together, we can share a good laugh or a good cry. We can walk with someone through a difficult season or share their joy in a joyous season. As the body of Christ, this is part of our calling and responsibility.

These are tumultuous times in which we live. More and more people in the body are suffering because of the things happening in the world, and more and more nonbelievers are seeking hope, help, and refuge. This is the time that we are supposed to be meeting more!

The enemy has found or utilized an excellent way to diminish our power as a body. Many people now watch preaching and teaching on the internet or TV. This is a great thing when used the right way, but the enemy has convinced some that they don't need to meet with others because they can get their needs met through these various other options. I have news for you, church on TV is not enough!

You miss out on things that happen before the recording begins. You miss out on things more powerful like corporate prayer and worship. The opportunity for God to use you to help in the body is lost for that moment. You can't get a hug or direct personal needs met because you aren't physically meeting with people. You're meeting with an electronic device that just cannot compare or substitute. God uses people, but if we aren't around people, we can't experience that.

Maybe you aren't currently connected to a church body because you haven't found one near you or one that is a fit. I strongly encourage you to keep looking. Don't give up. With the internet, there's little excuse to not find one. Perhaps you work an atypical work schedule. In that case, find a weekday or weeknight service or a Bible study group. You can even start your own Bible study group. Whatever you do, be sure you are connected, studying, and growing with other believers. This is a vital part of the Christian walk; if it wasn't, it wouldn't be mentioned in the Bible. For those of you that are connected and meeting regularly, invite others to join you and don't take for granted what you have.

Lord, I come humbly before You today asking that You strengthen and connect Your body. Help us to truly connect with one another and not give up on meeting together. I ask that You open the door to an appropriate meeting for those in Your body that aren't currently meeting and that they will feel Your presence and welcome You. Help me to understand the importance of and value in meeting. I pray this in Jesus' name. Amen.

WEEKEND CHALLENGE

Fix Your Face

Do you struggle in showing emotion? Perhaps you're at the opposite end of the spectrum and openly show emotions, even those that are inappropriate. Ask God to help you fix your face this weekend.

Make an intentional and conscientious effort to share a smile with at least 10 people each day. Want an even bigger challenge? Compete with yourself and see if you can break your record the next day, and the next, and the next. OK, you get the idea! Before you know it, smiling will be a habit for you.

Do you need an even deeper challenge? Smile at someone that you may have a difficult relationship with. Smile at this person each and every time you see them for the next two months. Don't give up! I know this is a challenge, but more than likely, this person's behavior toward you will change for the better. Better still, your heart towards them may soften as well and you are more likely to see them through the eyes of Christ!

Passion for Christ

God is so passionately in love with you that He sent His only Son to be abused and hurt beyond comprehension, and die a brutal death for you. Jesus Christ has so much passion for you that He willingly went through it all for you.

On a scale of 1-10, where would you say your passion for Christ is? Be honest with yourself. No one else needs to know because this is just between you and your Savior. How do you show your passion? Do you spend time regularly in the Word and chatting with Him? How about fleeing from sin? Are you serving Him by serving others? Do you share your passion and explain it to non-believers?

Take a moment to examine these things. In what ways do you show passion for Jesus? In what areas can you improve on this? Focus on the area that can use some improvement. Pray, and really seek God's face for a divine strategy on how you can improve in this area. Spend your weekend focusing on such improvement and use that strategy.

Joy in the Lord

One source of joy in the Lord is through our
service to others. But I will rejoice even if I lose my life,
pouring it out like a liquid offering to God,
just like your faithful service is an offering to God.
And I want all of you to share that joy.

PHILIPPIANS 2:17 NLT

Personally, I find that my greatest joy typically comes when the Lord is using me through my service to others. Whether it be praying for someone, serving in the church, feeding the homeless, or serving at a pregnancy center, etc. I find great joy in Him using me.

Where do you find joy? Do you currently serve in and out of the church? This weekend I challenge you to discover new joy through service. Maybe you are already serving in and out of the church, but I challenge you to serve in a new way this weekend. If you typically visit nursing homes, find a worthy organization that serves youth or children, and become a volunteer. If you usually serve in the church, serve by feeding the homeless. Do something that is out of your norm.

The possibilities are endless! By doing something different, not only are you serving a different group, but you may discover new gifts, interests, talents, joy, and even make new friends. If you need help with this challenge, I encourage you to contact the GLAD Mission. The people there would be happy to serve you and get you serving others!

Respect, Empathy, Compassion

Which people group did you choose to pray for this week? Did God move on your heart? Perhaps the Lord planted new ideas in your heart to serve that people group. Maybe not. Either is OK. I can help you with that too.

There are many ways to serve. Below is a list of ideas, but it is far from exhaustive. Remember that sometimes our service is through our finances as well.

Homeless

Give a homeless person money for food, give them food, or better yet, take some time and take them for a hot meal at a nearby restaurant and get to know them.

Persecuted Christians

Donate funds to "Voice of the Martyrs." Sign up for their updates or send an encouraging note to a persecuted Christian or missionary that you may know that is serving in a hostile environment.

Prisoners

Contact Angel Tree to learn of the various capacities in which you can serve and choose the one that's right for you, or search out a local prison ministry if you desire to serve more directly.

Gathering Together

This challenge may be seen by many as controversial, but we as Christians really need to get out of the box and extend beyond our comfort zones. I encourage you to visit a new church this weekend. The purpose of this challenge is not to get you to leave your present church (if you have one), but rather to get you to connect with other believers outside of your normal circle. It can be the same denomination that you are used to, or it can be one that you have little to no experience with as long as it's Christian. Go online to the church's website and read their statement of faith to be sure that it is indeed a Christian church first.

The purpose of this challenge is to get you to connect with other believers. Expect to experience something different. The church you visit may be louder or quieter than what you're used to. They will likely do things differently than what you are used to as well. This challenge will give you the opportunity to see and appreciate some of the differences in the body of Christ. It is my prayer that if you don't currently have a church that you call your own that you will discover one through this challenge. Whether it's through the process of exploring online and later visiting other churches, or if the church you visit this weekend is the one.

LIFE

IS A

PLAY

It's Not its Length,
but its Performance
That Counts

PREMATURE LOSS

I WAS RECENTLY ASKED BY SOMEONE WHAT I THOUGHT about premature death. My answer may shock you. As a Christian, I don't believe in premature death. I honestly believe the term came about because of senseless murders, babies dying at birth, and children dying from cancer. It's mankind's way of trying to explain, understand, and grapple with something that's bigger than us and clearly unexplainable.

You see, our tiny, finite minds can't possibly begin to understand all of God's purposes in a thing. That doesn't mean that I'm not saddened by such a loss, but the truth is my ways are not His ways. **Read Isaiah 55:8.**

Let's examine what sometimes happens through the life of a child that dies from cancer. Yes, the end outcome is terrible from an earthly perspective, but truth be told, that child is now in a better place being in heaven. It really stinks how much they had to suffer to get there though, and that's not to mention what friends and family go through.

Many times these children manage to maintain their joy despite their pain. I'd have to say that God granted them grace for that. Lots of good things can come from bad situations, even terrible deaths such as in this scenario.

More often than not, family, friends, and sometimes even entire communities band together and rally around the child and their family. Relationships are mended, wounds healed, hearts softened either by being part of the rally or by having a close and direct encounter with the child. Sometimes souls are even saved, due to something a dying child has said or done.

> And we know that in all things
> God works for the good of those who love him,
> who have been called according to his purpose.

ROMANS 8:28 NIV

We can't possibly see or begin to understand all the lives any one situation or person may touch. Whether good or bad in our eyes at the time, God is still going to work it all together for our good. It may take time for us to see it and realize it, or we may not see it at all in our lifetime. It's a blessing and a precious gift when we do get to see it though.

My point is this, with God in control, having created us for a purpose and working things together for the good of those who love Him, how can any death be premature? Even in a lost pregnancy or stillbirth, there was a purpose in that life. Purpose fulfilled. Do you really think that God is going to snuff out the life of one of His beloved creations before its purpose has been fulfilled?

There can be no such thing as premature death. We only think a death is premature because the person was so young and had their "whole life" ahead of them or because they were so young that they hadn't yet experienced life. Well, dare I say that "yes" they have their whole life ahead of them, and they get to spend it in eternity! Technically, they are better off than we are.

> My times are in your hands;
> deliver me from my enemies
> and from those who pursue me.

PSALM 31:15 NIV

With our times in His hands, we can rest assured that no death, including our own, will ever be premature. What we should be concerned about is how we live our life; not the hour of our death.

> Therefore keep watch, because you
> do not know the day or the hour.

MATTHEW 25:13 NIV

This goes for us as well as for our friends and loved ones. That's one of the many reasons that we are instructed to quickly forgive and not let the sun go down on our anger. We aren't promised tomorrow, or even a moment from now. Nobody is.

We need to live each day as if it is our first as well as our last. Our first because it's a new day and a gift (that's why it's called the present) and our last because we never know when it will end. We don't want to die with regrets or leave others with regrets.

Is there anything the Lord is impressing on you to make right in your life today? Maybe it's something you've promised to do but haven't done it yet. Could it be that you need to make amends with someone? Perhaps there's something you need to start or stop doing. There's no time like now. Tomorrow's not promised, so do that thing now!

Heavenly Father, please help me to understand that there's no such thing as premature death and that my hours and minutes are numbered. Help me to heal from _____ (fill in the blank) that I considered a premature loss. Please show me Your hand at work in that situation. Help me to live each day as if it is my first and last. I ask this in the mighty name of Jesus. Amen.

PRACTICE WHAT
YOU PREACH

READ MATTHEW 24:36-50. IT IS MADE VERY CLEAR THAT WE have no idea when our time is going to be up. Either we will die, or Jesus will return, but we really don't know when. We are warned to keep watch, or always be prepared.

This section of Scripture perfectly aligns with this fortune. **Go back and read Matthew 24:44-50 again.** Go ahead, you know I'll wait! OK, so we know that we need to be faithful and wise servants. We can't be hypocrites. How do we do that?

We are to practice what we claim to believe. Service is one of those things that are required. We aren't talking about working or serving your way into heaven. Don't get it twisted!

What good is it, my brothers,
if a man claims to have faith but has no deeds?
Can such faith save him?

JAMES 2:14 NIV

But someone will say, "You have faith; I have deeds."
Show me your faith without deeds,
and I will show you my faith by my deeds.

JAMES 2:18 NIV

I'm sure you've probably heard the old saying, " Actions speak louder than words." That's exactly what the passage James 2:14-26 is talking about! We are supposed to live and walk out our faith through action and deed, not just fancy speech. Be about something and do it!

We can't merely show up to church on Sunday to hear a Word preached and think that that's all we need to do. We have to be about it. We must live it and breathe it, just like a professional athlete is with their sport. To have a general head knowledge of our "faith" isn't enough. We must live it, breathe it, and be about it. That means having a working knowledge of what we hear, read, learn and by actually doing it!

It's simply not enough to say and know that we should love one another. We need to put action to our words! You know that you are supposed to quickly forgive, but do you really do that? I'm not saying that we have to be perfect. We never will be, but through the power of the Holy Ghost, we can live a life that shows our faith rather than just talking about it.

It's not how long we live that matters. What matters is the kind of life we live. Do you really want to be known for how old you were when you died, or would you rather leave a legacy? If you were to die tomorrow, what would you be remembered for? What would people say about you or call you? Would they say you are selfish and greedy or giving and generous? Loving or hateful? Forgiving or vengeful?

Today I have an unusual activity for you. You may think it's odd, but it does have a purpose. Trust me! Create a list of at least 5-10 ways people would describe you or something they would say about you at your funeral if you were to die today? Be brutally honest with yourself. Were you able to come up with at least three positive things? Awesome! That shows areas you are doing well in. Chances are, anything that didn't make it on that list has room for improvement. Remember, none of us is perfect, but we are all to strive to be like Jesus and live what we believe.

Lord, help me to live in such a way that people see my faith in action. Help me to not be a hypocrite, always speaking but not doing. Please empower me to live a life that is a holy and pleasing sacrifice to You. I want to be more like You Jesus, but I know that I can't do it on my own. Help me! In Jesus' name, I pray. Amen.

AGAPE LOVE, PART 1

READ 1 CORINTHIANS 13. YES, READ THE WHOLE CHAPTER. It's only 13 verses. I'll try to make this devotion shorter for you.

After reading that you probably know what today is about. Love! It's about God's real and unconditional love.

> Now these three remain: faith, hope, and love.
> But the greatest of these is love.

1 CORINTHIANS 13:13 HCSB

1 Corinthians chapter 13 is the definition of the godly love that we are to strive to operate in every day. It's the gold standard if you will. More than that, it is the standard that we are supposed to use with everyone.

> For if you love those who love you,
> what reward will you have?
> Don't even the tax collectors do the same?

MATTHEW 5:46 HCSB

In the Holman Christian Standard Bible, love is even called, "the superior way." God intends for us to love all people. That doesn't mean we have to love their actions or their sins. Not everyone has the same capacity as you.

You will find people in the world with a greater and lesser capacity to both sin and love. In other words, some people will sin more than you and some less in particular areas, and some will love greater than you and others less. Keep in mind the only perfect person is Jesus, and we are to do our best to be like Him.

1 Corinthians 13 shows us that our motives are more important than our actions. It's all about the condition of our heart. That is what God is ultimately looking at. What's your heart's condition? Is it hardened or bitter, or is it soft and tender towards others?

People often think that it doesn't matter how we treat people that we don't know, particularly people that are supposed to be serving us. We need to challenge that mindset right now! It is not OK to be short with the grocery store clerk, rude to a waitress, or impatient with a nurse. We are to love everyone, and if you really think about it, these people deserve to be loved and possibly need it shown to them even more. After all, not only are they serving us, but they're dealing with others that disrespect them or worse. How do you treat people you don't know? Do you treat them differently than the people closest to you?

Sometimes people are the other way around, being nicer to outsiders than those closest to them. Perhaps you are one of those people. One of the many reasons for this is that we expect more of those closest to us or we feel too comfortable with them. We need to be careful not to take advantage of them, and be sure to treat them with the same godly love. Isn't that how we want to be treated? Our lives aren't about how long they are, but what we do with them!

Lord, please help me to see and love others as You do. Help me to treat people in a way that is honoring and acceptable to You. I thank You for the people You've placed in my life, and I ask that You show me how to best show them Your love. Help me to reflect You to them. Let people see You in me. Help me to lead others to You through godly love. In Jesus' name, amen.

AGAPE LOVE, PART 2

If I gave everything I have to the poor and even sacrificed my body, I could boast about it; but if I didn't love others, I would have gained nothing.

1 CORINTHIANS 13:13 HCSB

THIS SCRIPTURE CONFIRMS THIS WEEK'S FORTUNE IN MY mind. It's not about length, but it's also not just about what we do in life. Our life is about how we do what we do. A person can give food to a homeless person, but how much more powerful is it if that person stops to pray with them and talk to them in godly love?!

Let's look at what love is and is not.

LOVE IS...	LOVE IS NOT...
patient	jealous
kind	bragging
forgiving (no record of wrong)	proud
joyful in truth	irritable
faithful	rude
hopeful	demanding its own way
enduring	giving up

The short of it is that love is not selfish, is focused on others, and is Christ-like. Love is supernatural! Without the help of the Holy Spirit, we can't love the way Christ did. Love goes against what our flesh and the world tells us. It isn't self-serving, but rather it's all about serving others.

All of us have some aspects of love that we exemplify better than others. Grab a sheet of paper and list them. Likewise, we also have aspects that we truly struggle with. Now create a second column like I did here and list those as well. Make sure you are looking at what love *is* and what it *is not*. For example, if you struggle with jealousy or irritability, you would list those under your "Struggles" column.

I think that the challenge many of us may face is the fact that we are to treat all people with love. Matthew was very clear (in Matthew 5:46) that it doesn't mean as much to love those that we find easy to love as it is to love those that we find more difficult to love. In other words, it's easier to love someone that loves us back.

I believe that God has given us people that love us to show us how we are supposed to love those that aren't so easy to love. If life is a play, then the whole world is a stage! We can learn from anyone anywhere. Sometimes we learn from people closest to us, and other times (due to books and current technology) we learn from people we don't know that are half a world away from us. Our examples of how to love can be from different eras as well.

On your piece of paper, list the people that have taught you to love. You may list people like Jesus, Paul, Mother Theresa, my mom, my great aunt, and so on. List those that are the strongest examples of godly love to you. Now let's pray.

Dear Heavenly Father, I thank You for the people that You have blessed me with as an example of godly love and those that You have called me to love. Lord, please help me to love better. Increase Your love in me, and help me with the areas that I struggle with (read them from your list) when it comes to love. I want to be able to love the people in my life that others would call unlovable. I want to be more like You, but I need Your help! I ask these things in Jesus' name. Amen.

SALT AND LIGHT

You are the salt of the earth. But if the salt
should lose its taste, how can it be made salty?
It's no longer good for anything but to be
thrown out and trampled on by men.

MATTHEW 5:13 HCSB

WE ARE CALLED TO BE SALT AND LIGHT. WE ARE SUPPOSED TO give a good flavor to life through our actions and example. People watch other people, and they pay attention when you least expect it. When you live a life that consistently shines and gives good flavor you are an example for others to follow.

What do I mean by good flavor? I'm glad you asked. You've probably heard people make comments about people, places, or situations saying that they left a "bad taste" in their mouth. Well, we want to leave a good taste and be a godly example that people will look to, want, and want to copy.

Read Matthew 5:13-16 in your favorite Bible translation. It's not too long; I'll wait. I don't know about you, but I don't want to lose my taste/flavor, and I certainly don't want to be thrown out or trampled on! We as Christians should not leave a bad taste in someone's mouth through our interactions. People should desire to be around us more because they want more of that good taste.

Sure, we know that we are supposed to be the salt and the light, but how do we do that? A true love for Christ overflows into a true love for people. When we are focused on Christ we see things differently, both people and situations. We long to serve Him and obey Him. The way that we treat people on an everyday basis is different from the way others behave.

Christians are to be a glowing example. Others should see Christ-like behavior in us on a regular basis. Our light shines before men. People want to be around us and be like us, because we inspire them to see, be, and do good.

What does that look like for you? Are people drawn to you? Do you give and serve freely? Do you treat others with love and respect, putting their needs above your own?

This doesn't mean that you are to be a doormat though. You're also not supposed to neglect yourself, but at the same time sacrifice is not a bad thing. Everyone needs to learn their own balance with sacrifice and self-care. The Holy Spirit, if we allow, instructs us on how, when, and what to give.

Some people, myself included, are givers and can get frustrated because they want to give or do more than they are currently able. Trust that God sees and knows their heart and blesses them and their ability to do and give in the future. Like God, plenty of people can spot fake or false motives. It's the condition of our heart that matters most when it comes to serving and giving.

> Each person should do as he has decided
> in his heart-not out of regret or out of necessity,
> for God loves a cheerful giver.

2 CORINTHIANS 9:7 HCSB

Make no mistake on this. Serving is giving. When you serve in whatever capacity, you are giving of your time, talent, and self. Serving is our greatest opportunity to shine. When we serve are we doing it in love, with a cheerful heart and a smile on our face? Or are we serving out of a sense of obligation? If we are not cheerful in our giving and serving, we need to reexamine our heart.

In giving, we should feel joy. I would venture to say that if you don't feel joy when you are serving, then it is quite likely that you are serving in the wrong place or capacity. Reevaluate your service. Are you joyful when you serve? Does it bring a smile to your face? Are others happy to be served by you, with you, or inspired by your service?

Ask yourself the above questions and be honest with yourself. Was there a point that service was joyful, but then, later on, you found yourself drained of that joy? If so, try to pinpoint when that joy was lost. Think of other places or positions that you could serve in that you would enjoy. Remember that God created each of us to be different. You may enjoy cleaning, while another person may enjoy clerical work, and yet another person enjoys counseling people. All of these roles are equally necessary. Don't try to fit somewhere that you don't belong, but rather let the Holy Spirit direct you to the place and position that you do belong. You will serve best and find joy when you are in the right space and place!

Father God, I come to You with a pure and humble heart that longs to serve and delight You. Thank You for the many blessings You have given me and for the ability to give and serve. Lord, please increase that ability, and if I'm in the wrong place or position, please lead me to where I can best serve You. Lead me to the place that You designed for me. I ask this in the mighty name of Jesus. Amen.

WEEKEND CHALLENGE

First and Last

How does one live each day as if it is their first and last? Well, let's start with first. We know that God's mercies are new every morning (Lamentations 3:22-23). We start every day fresh and new. Today is the first day of the rest of your life. It's a fresh new opportunity. What can you do new or different, and with a fresh perspective?

We never know what day will be our last, because tomorrow isn't promised (Proverbs 27:1 and James 4:13-14). In order to get the most out of our lives, we need to get the most we can out of each and every day. How? It's all about perspective. If you can truly start each day fresh putting down past failures, problems, regrets, and sorrows and see each day as new and an opportunity for greatness then we are better able to achieve that greatness. To live each day as our last means that we are intentional in what we do and don't do, living consciously aware of our actions, the world around us, and the impact that our actions have on the world around us.

The challenge for this weekend is to change your perspective. At least for this weekend make a conscious effort to live each day as though it is your first and last, no regrets. Nobody is perfect, but I challenge you to try and carry it on past this weekend and doing it every day. Some days you'll be more successful than others, but you will achieve a greater life, getting more out of it every day when you can change your perspective.

Life Application

What is God calling you to do? What are your beliefs about what God expects from you and your life? Are you still trying to figure out what God is calling you to do?

We know that we are called to love and quickly forgive. These are things that all believers are required to do, but we each have our own callings and assignments. Are you clueless as to what God may be wanting you to do? Today's challenge is going to address that for you!

Take your pen and paper and divide the paper into two sections. Label one section "Irritations" and the other "Passions." Now, I want you to think about your stand on social issues. For things or people groups that you have a strong passion for write these things in the "Passion" section. What problems irritate you or grate on your nerves? Write these in the "Irritation" section.

Pray about what you've written in each section. Ask the Lord to point out the area or areas that He would have you focus. Once you've determined those areas, research them a bit. Where and how might you get connected and serve or give? The resources in the back of this book may help.

Look Deeper at Godly Love

This challenge may end up being your hardest one yet! Who is your love mentor? Who taught you to love like Christ? Is your person from this era? Are they someone close to you or someone you know well?

Sometimes part of loving someone is building them up. If your person is from this era, and especially if it's not someone you're super close to, write that person a letter. Pour out your heart to them, let them know how they've shaped you, and how much you appreciate them. Make sure they get this letter in whatever form possible. You don't have to, but you might even want to send a special gift with it.

Now think of that person in your life that is difficult to love, and you don't "feel" love for them. Maybe it's a boss, co-worker, or neighbor. Go out of your way today to bless that person. It may be a cup of coffee, a small gift card, or other "just because" gift you think they'd appreciate or doing a small task for them.

Focus on Love

Which group of people do you struggle with showing God's love consistently? Is it those close to you, or outsiders? Do you find it difficult to love others at all?

With the help of the Lord do a full evaluation on how you love others. Ask Him for help in this area. How and where can you improve?

Some suggestions may include praying for, paying attention to, interacting with, and even complimenting an outsider that you take for granted. I know of one family that did this, and they got to know their trash collector. They even took it a step further one day and sat out one sunny morning waiting for them to give them a six pack of their favorite soda! That was a glowing example of godly love.

The Lord may put it on your heart to do something similar. Perhaps He'll have you go out of your way for the gas station clerk on your way to work or someone else that regularly serves you, but you looked past or have treated poorly. On the other hand, your issue may lie with loved ones. Should that be the case, do something special and unexpected for them. Your challenge is to focus on loving others.

Be a Glowing Example

Who can you mentor? You didn't get to where you are right now without help somewhere along the line. Is there a new mom in your church or a babe in Christ? Do you know of a teenager that lives on your street? In the case of teens, it's a good idea to know and work with their parents as well.

Sure, this challenge may stretch you beyond your comfort zone, but that's the point and is OK. We aren't here to be comfortable! Pray about who it is that you are to be mentoring and pray for that person.

You may be asking how mentoring works. Get involved in that person's life to the degree that they allow. Show them godly love and be a glowing example for them. When they are struggling with something, share your experience and open up to them. Be transparent and encourage them. A quick, easy summary would be to teach, encourage, and pray. Begin a mentoring relationship today!

Life to You
is a

DASHING

AND BOLD

ADVENTURE

ADVENTURE
IN SURRENDER

IN CASE YOU HADN'T NOTICED, A LOT OF THINGS IN THIS LIFE (when it comes to our Christian walk) are paradoxical. We die to live, receive from giving, and there's freedom in surrender. These are just a few, but today we are going to talk about surrender. Did you know that there's adventure in surrender?

OK, so maybe it's another paradox, but it is very much true! When we die to the flesh and fully surrender, our lives do become a dashing and bold adventure. Let's look at surrender first, and then we can look at the resulting adventure.

> "Abba, Father," he cried out, "everything is
> possible for you. Please take this cup
> of suffering away from me.
> Yet I want your will to be done, not mine."
>
> **MARK 14:36 NLT**

Just like everything else, we should look to Jesus for our example. He knew that He was in for the worst agony, even beyond imagination. Yet, He was completely submitted to the Father's will. He was willing to endure the horrendous suffering. How many of us can say the same?

True surrender is taking our hands off of things. We need to maintain a hands-off approach to our lives and openly, readily accept God's solutions and directions. This is real surrender. We can't control; we have to submit to His control.

> For through the law I have died to the law,
> that I might live to God. I have been crucified with
> Christ; and I no longer live, but Christ lives in me.
> The life I now live in the flesh, I live by faith in the
> Son of God, who loved me and gave Himself for me.

GALATIANS 2:19-20 HCSB

We are crucified with Christ. It's no longer our life anyway. We are to be submitted to Him, and live by faith; no longer in the flesh. I know that there are times that it is easier said than done. We were never promised an easy life, just an eternal reward. Christ lives in us though, making it all possible even when it seems impossible.

The real adventure comes in our letting go of control. The adventure lies in following God's lead and trusting in His timing even though you don't know where you'll end up or when. The excitement lies in trusting God and expecting a miracle even when you don't know the what, how, when, or even the why. It's not for us to know or fully understand, though He will occasionally bless us with this knowledge. Great missionaries have experienced these things. If you read about and study some of the greats, you will see a common thread. They didn't know how God would work things out, but they trusted that He would. Even in extreme and desperate circumstances, they did nothing in their power to influence the situation, unless you count prayer. Prayer invited God into the situation to have His way. That, of course, is another act of surrender. In every situation, God showed up and showed out in mighty ways for His people of great faith. These missionaries often spoke of excitement and risk in their lives. I don't know about you, but if I'm going to be taking risks, I certainly don't want to be doing it without God!

When we surrender our will to His, we allow Him to work miracles through us. When we operate in the flesh, we block those miracles because we try to take credit for what God has done through us because we did some work. Do you want miracles? Surrender your will to Christ today. The adventure lies in not knowing the details of how, when, where, or why, but in completely trusting Him and His protection, peace, power, presence, and provision. Yes, it can be scary at times, but you will be filled with peace about it because you know He'll work it out even better than you imagined. It is exciting to see what God does when we simply get out of the way!

What do you need to relinquish control of and surrender to God?

Dear Heavenly Father, I want to live the adventurous life of surrender. Show me how to truly let go and give you full control. Increase my faith that I may walk by faith and not by sight. I know that I don't have to be some great missionary to experience these things in my life, but show me how I can apply this knowledge to my life. I ask this in the precious name of Jesus. Amen.

DYING TO SELF

If you try to hang on to your life, you will lose it.
But if you give up your life for my sake,
you will save it. And what do you benefit if you
gain the whole world but lose your own soul?
Is anything worth more than your soul?

MATTHEW 16:25-26 NLT

He Himself bore our sins in His body
on the tree, so that, having died to sins,
we might live for righteousness;
by His wounding you have been healed.

1 PETER 2:24 HCSB

AS CHRISTIANS WE DIE TO OURSELVES, BUT WHAT DOES THAT mean? It means that we die to habitual sin and strive to live right. We live our lives with eternity in mind; knowing that we are only here for a little while. Our lives on earth are just a speck in comparison to all eternity.

People of the world, those without Christ, seek to gain whatever they can in the world and to meet the needs and desires of their flesh. Most of them don't even know that it is to the detriment of their very soul. That is why we are required to share the gospel. When we lead a person to Christ, we are literally helping to save their life, their eternal life. No, we aren't the One that saves it, but rather God allows us to be a part of it. That is a privilege and honor, and it's pretty exciting.

So Jesus said to the Jews who had believed Him,
"If you continue in My word, you really are My disciples.

JOHN 8:31 HCSB

Of course, dying to ourselves is a daily process. One must read the Bible regularly, and not just read it, but study it with the help of other books too. It's not enough to just read. We must seek to understand, apply what we learn, and do what it says.

He must increase, but I must decrease.

JOHN 3:30 HCSB

We need to allow God to increase in us. We do this by living the Word, and not just reading it. We also decrease through our humility. When we give God the glory for something, He has graced us to do or be a part of He increases while we decrease. We have to maintain our focus on Christ and not our own achievements.

It takes a certain level of boldness to claim Christ in our victories. He is our source of victory. When God does something awesome in, through, or for you, do you give Him all the glory? Do you make it known to others that it was because of God?

Father God, I come before You wanting You to increase in my life and Your help in dying to my flesh. Stir up the holy fire inside of me. Create a raging inferno; that I hunger and thirst for You instead of the things of this world. Please increase my boldness to share You with others and give You all the glory. I ask for these things in the matchless name of Jesus. Amen.

ALIVE IN CHRIST

What shall we say, then? Shall we go on sinning
so that grace may increase? By no means!
We died to sin; how can we live in it any longer?
Or don't you know that all of us who were
baptized into Christ Jesus were baptized into
his death? We were therefore buried with him
through baptism into death so that, just as
Christ was raised from the dead through the
glory of the Father, we too may live a new life.

ROMANS 6:1-4 NIV

For the wages of sin is death, but the gift of God
is eternal life in Christ Jesus our Lord.

ROMANS 6:23 NIV

AS BELIEVERS, WE ARE TO LIVE A NEW LIFE; NO LONGER
embedded in sin. We need to remember that there are
sins of commission and sins of omission. Sins of commission are a bit more obvious because that is when
we do something that we shouldn't such as lie, cheat,

or steal. A sin of omission isn't as noticeable to us. That is when we don't do something that we know we should such as forgiving someone.

So, what does it mean to be alive in Christ? It's more than just being dead to sin. It's being in love with Him, and when you love someone, you naturally want to express that love and spend time with them. What do you do to express that love?

We know that faith without works is dead. I'm going to take this in a new direction that you may or may not have considered before. Love without demonstration is also dead. When was the last time you allowed God to interrupt your life, plans, or agenda? These all belong to Him, but yet we still try to maintain total control. That's why we get frustrated or angry when times get hard because things are out of control!

Do you want to live a life that is a dashing and bold adventure? Let the Holy Spirit guide you and interrupt you in your day to day life. Have you ever seen someone and you suddenly felt like you were supposed to talk to them, pray with them, or give them something? Or maybe you suddenly felt like you were supposed to take a different route to work or to go somewhere you hadn't planned. What did you do in those or similar situations, and what was the outcome? These are examples of God interrupting or being led by the Spirit.

I've had increasing experience with this. It really is bold and exciting when you obey. I've been spared from serious accidents, made great connections, and even been used to bless people; and that's not counting those that have accepted Christ. I've been on some awesome adventures because I've allowed myself to be led by the Holy Spirit. This book you're holding is a great example. I would never have done it on my own!

I will admit that at one time, even though I was saved, I lived my life happily in my own little bubble. The adventure is now much better and worth any cost! The Lord wants to use and bless you, and stretch you beyond your comfort zone. Will you allow Him? Come on out of that box, and be alive in Christ!

Heavenly Father, I thank You, and I praise You for all that You are, all that You've done, and all that You desire to do in, through, and for me. I ask that You help me to be more sensitive to Your lead and to respond quickly in obedience. Help me to live a life that is a bold and dashing adventure for Your glory. In Jesus' name, amen.

OBEDIENCE

But Samuel replied, "What is more
pleasing to the LORD: your burnt offerings
and sacrifices or your obedience to his voice?
Listen! Obedience is better than sacrifice,
and submission is better than offering
the fat of rams.

1 SAMUEL 15:22 NLT

And so, dear brothers and sisters,
I plead with you to give your bodies to God
because of all he has done for you. Let them be
a living and holy sacrifice-the kind he will find
acceptable. This is truly the way to worship him.

ROMANS 12:1 NLT

OBEDIENCE IS BETTER THAN SACRIFICE, BUT OUR BODIES ARE
a living sacrifice. How can this be? When we live a
life of obedience, loving one another, forgiving, not
self-centered, etc. we are a pleasing, living sacrifice
for the Lord. Obedience is a key part of it, and the

Bible tells us how to do it. Yes, we are saved by grace and faith, but as Christians, we become new creatures that are no longer self-absorbed and consumed by sin.

Always be joyful. Never stop praying.
Be thankful in all circumstances,
for this is God's will for you who belong to Christ Jesus.
Do not stifle the Holy Spirit.
Do not scoff at prophecies,
but test everything that is said.
Hold on to what is good.
Stay away from every kind of evil.

1 THESSALONIANS 5:16-22 NLT

Our joy comes from the Lord, and when we live a prayerful and thankful life, we have that joy. To never stop praying doesn't mean that we should lock ourselves in our prayer closet and never come out again. It also doesn't mean that we can just pray about everything and never take any kind of action. There will be times that praying is all we are supposed to do, and times that the Holy Spirit will lead us to action. We should live a life of prayer, turning to God in all circumstances. That means turning to Him first in situations large and small. This can be difficult since we often want to turn to another human being.

Being thankful in all circumstances can be a challenge when you're in a rough season in life, but it's much easier if you've already made it a habit during an easier season. To be thankful in every situation means that you can maintain a proper perspective, finding things that are positive and remembering who God is. This brings the joy of the Lord.

We all must be careful not to hold back the Holy Spirit. This is a major part of being obedient. When the Holy Spirit leads you to do something you need to do it. You'll know when it's the Holy Spirit if you're living a connected, godly life. This also means not discouraging or stopping another person from doing something if the Spirit is leading them. For instance, if a friend is led to join a missionary team traveling to Iraq, you should pray for and with them, encouraging them to follow God's lead. It can be hard enough to be obedient. They don't need to hear from you how dangerous it is, or any other negative opinions. They need encouragement to trust and obey.

When someone comes to you saying the Lord told me this or that it is unwise to just blindly hold to whatever they say. You also shouldn't just completely discard it. Instead, take it to the Lord in prayer, and hold on to what is good and true. Do not embrace evil.

When we truly submit to God, living our lives as a sacrifice for Him, and following His lead, our lives will be an adventure. We will be blessed to see prayer answered in amazing ways. We'll see God's mighty hand at work in our lives and the lives of others. If we allow, the confines of our comfort zones will be removed as we step out in faith doing things we never thought possible!

Daddy God, I just thank You for all the wonderful things You've given me, but especially for Your gifts of salvation and the Holy Spirit. Please help me to live a life of obedience that is a pleasing and acceptable sacrifice to You. Increase my faith that I may step outside of the box of my comfort zone to live fully for You. I ask this in the mighty name of Jesus. Amen.

CHRISTIAN WALK

And this is love: that we walk according
to His commands. This is the command
as you have heard it from the beginning:
you must walk in love.

2 JOHN 1:6 HCSB

THERE'S AN OLD SAYING THAT STATES, "YOU CATCH MORE FLIES with honey." In other words, you have a better chance of turning a situation around when you are loving. Christians can't be mean and hateful and expect to draw others to Christ, but that also doesn't mean that we should compromise the gospel to show love or accommodate one's sins. Born-again believers must walk in love and the Word. In this book (2 John), John is giving a warning about false teachers.

Live such good lives among the pagans that,
though they accuse you of doing wrong,
they may see your good deeds
and glorify God on the day he visits us.

1 PETER 2:12 NIV

We have to do our absolute best with help from the Holy Spirit, and be completely dependent on, connected to, and obedient to God to live a life that is a godly example. It doesn't matter who sees us, but we need to make sure our walk is in obedience and an example for all. There have been witches and warlocks that have seen the error of their ways, repented, and turned to Christ because they watched a Christian's life over a long period and then got to know the person and Christ. How exciting that must be for the Christians that get to play a role in that!

The only way we can walk in the Word and not compromise the gospel is to spend time in it. You can't be a part of something you know nothing about. You won't likely be accurate in sharing or defending what's in the Bible if you don't even read it. Likewise, reading the Bible does nothing for you if you do nothing with what you've read. We need to be sharing the gospel. We are instructed to be doers of the Word.

Do not merely listen to the word, and so deceive
yourselves. Do what it says. Anyone who listens
to the word but does not do what it says
is like a man who looks at his face in a mirror and,
after looking at himself, goes away
and immediately forgets what he looks like.

JAMES 1:22-24 NIV

When we don't do what the Bible says, we forget it. Walking in love, turning from sin, and serving others is much more difficult. It takes both, listening (or reading) and doing to have a good, strong Christian walk.

He will repay each one according to his works.

ROMANS 2:6 HCSB

Some believers think that what they do in life doesn't really matter. Others think it's OK to just keep on sinning, doing whatever they want, and just go to church on Sundays. How's your Christian walk? Do you walk in love, spend time in the Word and with the Lord? Are you a doer?

Dear Heavenly Father, please help me to walk in love and be a doer of Your Word. I want my walk to be pleasing to You and an example for others. Help me in my areas of weakness and continue to build my strengths. I know that I can do nothing without You. That is why I come humbly before You asking these things in Jesus' name. Amen.

WEEKEND CHALLENGE

Adventurer

Has God put something in your heart that you've been too scared or stubborn to do? This thing may be something you've thought about recently, or it could be something that you've always wanted to do and haven't. Dare to become an adventurer! Pray about the thing and ask God to show you what you should do with that desire.

Perhaps you've always wanted to learn a language. You won't learn it by just wanting to do it though! You need to take a class. The internet has opened up the world of possibilities. You have a vast amount of choices to learn another language. Investigate your options such as taking a local class, an online class, or purchasing the software. Some people are self-motivated enough that they can do well with software, but others need the accountability that a live class provides. Know who you are and be honest with yourself. Choose the method that will most likely result in success for you.

Maybe you've always wanted to travel or do something else that seems cost prohibitive. Start researching that thing to get an actual idea of the cost. Sometimes things are easier to get than we think, but because we place such a high value on it, we assume others would too and that it must be too expensive and out of our reach. Once you have a price range, start saving for it. You've heard the old saying, "Out of sight, out of mind," so post reminders around your home in places that you'll see every day to help you stay motivated in your saving.

God often puts desires in our hearts to connect us with other people. It's not just for us even though it will bring us great pleasure or satisfaction. In taking a class, it may be to witness to someone in the class. Traveling may open your eyes to things in the world you once ignored, but are created to address. The purpose of this challenge is to get you to expand your thinking and take the limits off of God. Pray about your adventure regularly and become an adventurer!

Share Your Testimony

Back in the day churches used to have a time where people could share their testimony. Some churches are even bringing it back now. This is exciting to me because testimonies are so encouraging. It's rare that you hear people telling someone about something God has done for them.

Don't underestimate the power of your testimony. Take time to deliberately share your testimony this weekend and have conversations about God. Society allows us to brag about our kids, grandkids, dogs, accomplishments, and even the best pizza in town, but we need to be bragging about God. Brag about what He has done for you and what He can do for the person you are speaking to. You may even be able to lead them to Christ because of it!

Stretch

Have you ever prayed with a random stranger or felt like you were supposed to? Chances are the Holy Spirit was moving your heart. When was the last time you shared Christ with someone? Have you ever?

I'm not judging you by asking these questions, but these are some serious questions that we should be asking ourselves on a regular basis.

> Then He said to them, "Go into all the world and preach the gospel to the whole creation.
>
> **MARK 16:15 HCSB**

Most Christians are familiar with the Great Commission. But how many actually do it? Your challenge this weekend is to actively look for someone to strike up a conversation with and share the gospel. Here a few questions that may help you get started.

- "What is your faith background?"
- "Do you have a religious preference?"
- "Do you think you'll go to heaven when you die? Why?"
- "Do you believe in life after death?"
- "What do you believe happens to us when we die?"

I know that these questions may seem blunt and a bit awkward, but these questions are very effective if you know the answers yourself. A lot of people will say they believe they are going to heaven because they are a good person, haven't killed anyone, etc. This is a red flag for you that either no one has ever shared the gospel with them or that they don't understand it.

Some important things to remember during this challenge is that not all people will respond the same. Some will love to talk with you and others will not. Remember to speak to people with love and respect. Just keep in mind that if you are rejected, they aren't actually rejecting you. They are rejecting Christ, but you may have planted a seed.

Prayer Journal

Have you ever prayed a prayer and forgot what you prayed for? Or even worse, you received an answer to a prayer and forgot you even prayed for it? I've had that embarrassing situation happen to me when I was with a friend. A prayer was answered, I had forgotten ever praying for that thing, and when the answer came my friend had to remind me by saying, "Hey we prayed for this. Our prayers were answered! Praise God! Don't you remember?" Ouch! I had truthfully forgotten, but I did praise Him for answering our prayers.

There are many reasons to start and keep a prayer journal. One reason is to hopefully spare you from an embarrassing scenario like mine. Truthfully though, it is important to remember when God answers our prayers and to thank Him. It also helps us to know when and how He's answered us.

Like many activities in this book, it helps to increase your faith. All you have to do is go back periodically and re-read your answered prayers.

To keep a prayer journal, you can be as detailed as you'd like. Most people start with the date, a brief description of what or who is being prayed for, and the kind of prayer prayed. Then you go back when the prayer is answered, writing in the date, and a description of how God answered. Some people prefer writing more detailed descriptions and writing down exactly what they prayed.

Bookstores sell various types of journals, but you can even use a basic spiral notebook that you can pick up cheap during a back to school sale. Start a prayer journal if you haven't already. If you already have a prayer journal go back and read over it again. Revisit and re-evaluate some old prayers. Are they still important and unanswered? If so, go back and pray those prayers again, then revise them and improve upon them before praying them again. Maybe God has answered it already, but it was subtle. Update your journal accordingly.

Life Scripture

As we have discussed, a large part of our Christian walk is being doers of the Word. What scriptures or concepts are you walking out in your day to day life? Using a separate concordance or one in the back of your Bible, look up those scriptures and concepts. Which one are you doing best? Which one strikes a chord with you or jumps out at you? This is the one you are going to focus on this weekend.

Do something creative with this scripture that you've chosen. It can be as simple as writing it in your best handwriting on a piece of paper and decorating that paper. Or it can be more elaborate like carving it into a piece of wood and creating a plaque. You could even make a collage, paint, do metal work, or some other interesting work of art. God gave each of us a level of creativity. God is The Creator, and since we are made in His image, we are creators as well.

While you are creating your masterpiece with your chosen scripture, memorize it. Talk to God while you make it, and let Him guide you through the process. Once you are done creating it, find a suitable place in your home to display it, or you may be led to give it away as a gift.

YOU
WILL
SUCCEED

*in Whatever
Calling
You Adopt*

SPIRITUAL GIFTS

AS LONG AS YOU ARE FOLLOWING THE LORD'S DIRECTION, you will succeed in whatever calling you adopt. God will not call you to do something that He has not equipped, designed, and destined you to do. You have to adopt or accept that call though, and He will help you do it.

> We are confident of all of this because of our great trust in God through Christ. It is not that we think we are qualified to do anything on our own. Our qualification comes from God.
>
> **2 CORINTHIANS 3:4-5 NLT**

Our qualification is that we are saved. We are part of the Body of Christ. As part of the Body, with the Holy Spirit residing in us, we have spiritual gifts. These gifts are one of the ways that God equips us to do good works or the things He has called us to do.

There are times that we may feel inadequate or that we just can't do something that the Lord is leading us to do. That's actually not a bad place to be, even though it can feel like it. It's moments like these that are an opportunity to increase our faith.

> Each time he said, "My grace is all you need.
> My power works best in weakness." So now I am glad
> to boast about my weaknesses, so that the power
> of Christ can work through me. That's why I take
> pleasure in my weaknesses, and in the insults,
> hardships, persecutions, and troubles that I suffer
> for Christ. For when I am weak, then I am strong.

2 CORINTHIANS 12:9-10 NLT

It's in our moments of insecurity regarding our abilities that God can best use us. When we feel like we can't do something on our own, we are forced to rely completely on Him. It's when we are weak that He makes us strong.

> Having then gifts differing according to the grace
> that is given to us, let us use them: if prophecy, let us
> prophesy in proportion to our faith; or ministry, let us
> use it in our ministering; he who teaches, in teaching;
> he who exhorts, in exhortation; he who gives,
> with liberality; he who leads, with diligence;
> he who shows mercy, with cheerfulness.

ROMANS 12:6-7 NKJV

Chances are you know at least one Christian that is extra bubbly and seems to always have something encouraging to say. I would venture to say that person has the gift of exhortation. When we operate in our spiritual gifts, they tend to just flow because they become a part of who we are. The more we exercise or use our gift, the easier it flows and increases our faith. The gift, like a muscle, grows with use.

All believers have spiritual gifts, but not all believers know what their spiritual gifts are. With that being said, it is safe to say that not all Christians are operating in their gifts. They haven't realized all that God has given them. They aren't the only ones missing out though. The Body of Christ is missing out when believers aren't utilizing their gifts.

There are two crucial points to remember about using spiritual gifts. The gifts are intended to serve the Lord, being used to help the Body of Christ and lead people to Christ. They are not to be used for selfish, personal gain. The second thing to remember is that the spiritual gifts must be operated in love, or they lose their potency.

Do you know what your spiritual gifts are? Do you operate in them? There are many resources available on spiritual gifts in general, as well as specific gifts. There are numerous tests to help you discover what spiritual gifts you may have. You can talk to your pastor or other leaders in your church if you would like to learn more. Your friends or loved ones may even have an idea as to what some of your gifts are. Sometimes things are easier to see as an outsider looking in. You can also look at the resource list in the back of this book. Most importantly, pray and ask God to show you what gifts He wants you to be operating in right now.

Daddy God, please help me to recognize and best use the spiritual gifts You've given me to glorify Your name. I want to serve and please You. I want to introduce others to You. Help me to always operate in love and be a good example. Let others see you in me. I ask these things in the almighty name of Jesus. Amen.

JOY AND PEACE

THERE IS MUCH TO BE SAID ABOUT LIVING A LIFE FOR CHRIST. It is certainly an adventure. By living a life for Christ, we get to experience unspeakable joy and have peace that is beyond worldly understanding.

For the Kingdom of God is not a matter
of eating and drinking, but of righteousness,
peace, and joy in the Holy Spirit,
because anyone who serves Christ in this
way is pleasing to God and approved by men.

ROMANS 14:17-18 NIV

Our joy comes in serving the Lord. Current world thinking wouldn't believe that serving anyone could produce such joy. Yet living a life for Christ does just that!

Always be full of joy in the Lord.
I say it again-rejoice! Let everyone see that you
are considerate in all you do.
Remember, the Lord is coming soon.
Don't worry about anything; instead pray

about everything. Tell God what you need,
and thank him for all he has done.
Then you will experience God's peace,
which exceeds anything we can understand.
His peace will guard your hearts
and minds as you live in Christ Jesus.

PHILIPPIANS 4:4-7 NLT

When we are devoted to obedience and service to God, our focus is right where it needs to be. Frequently, our concerns are more about what God is concerned about. In this lifestyle, we are more reliant on help from the Holy Spirit and God's provision. Since it's a regular way of living. our dependence is natural, stress is easier to handle, thanking God and praying continually come rather automatically. Of course, this is a generalization, but I'm sure you get my point. When you live your life in this manner and totally focused on Christ, you have that unspeakable joy and peace that passes all understanding. It is totally awesome!

Have you ever been able to maintain your focus on Christ? When you find it difficult to do, you need to turn your worries into prayer. Look at all God has done for you, in you, and through you. Thank Him and give Him praise. Lay all your problems at His feet and bow down and worship Him. Shout, scream, run, dance, cry; just do whatever it takes to draw closer to God and lose those chains! I want you to experience that joy and peace.

Heavenly Father, help me to not only gain but maintain my focus on You. I want to experience the fullness of all You have for me. I don't want to be outside of Your will for my life. I need You to guide me and teach me. I want more of You and to remain close to You. Help me, Lord. In Jesus' name. Amen.

PUZZLE PIECES

TO SUCCEED IN WHATEVER CALLING YOU ADOPT MEANS THAT
you've answered God's calling. That does not necessarily mean that you are called to full-time ministry.
Often people refer to God's calling as a position in
ministry. This distorts things and can confuse people
if God is calling them into anything other than full-
time, church ministry. God has a calling for everyone,
but it may be in business or government instead of
church ministry for example. People also lose sight of
the general Christian responsibilities that belong to
all believers. Sometimes they even push things off
onto those in full-time ministry because they believe
it is the job of those in ministry instead of their own.

Not everyone can have a call to full-time ministry.
God doesn't put all of His eggs into one basket! It
would leave huge gaping holes. If no one was ever
called to government, there would be no Christian
influence regarding laws. This is just one simple
example, of course. Here's another one for you. Most
people who are lost or seeking are not likely to just

walk into a church on their own. Have you ever heard of marketplace ministers? These are people God has called to business. They have a Christian influence in the business arena, ministering to, and leading people to Christ within the scope of their daily living and work.

I want to encourage you. Please don't think that if your calling isn't full-time ministry or something in the world system with a big, fancy name or title, that you or your calling are less than. I want you to picture something with me for a moment. Imagine the entire world as a jigsaw puzzle, and each person is a piece. Each person has a place and purpose in the puzzle or big picture. Without that person or piece, the puzzle is incomplete. A city needs a trash collector just as much as it needs a policeman and a mayor. A school needs students just as much as it needs teachers and janitors. We all need to connect and work with other people that our piece fits with.

We can't force ourselves into a slot we weren't created for. Nobody else can push us into the wrong position either. It won't be a proper fit. Just like a puzzle piece can bend, break, or tear as a result, we can become damaged also. We need to be careful to answer our calling and not that of someone else. We must do our part to complete the picture.

> But in fact, God has arranged the parts in the body,
> every one of them, just as he wanted them to be.
> If they were all one part, where would the body be?
> As it is, there are many parts, but one body.

1 CORINTHIANS 12:18-20 NIV

When we are obedient to our calling, be it a homeschool parent or a college professor, a neurosurgeon or nurse's aide, a CEO or pastor, a librarian or engineer, we will be more successful. That is because we will then, typically, be and do what God has called and equipped us to be and do. We aren't pretending or trying to fit somewhere we don't belong.

And we know that in all things God works
for the good of those who love him,
who have been called according to his purpose.

ROMANS 8:28 NIV

Do you know your calling? You should always go to God first. Pray and ask Him to reveal your calling to you. Sometimes God uses people to reveal things to us. There is no shame in seeking godly counsel. Some people that may be able to help you are leaders in your church, godly friends, and family, or even a Christian life coach. Learn your calling, and then learn and accept the value of your calling. Your piece is valuable and important.

Father God, please help me to learn and accept my calling and its value. Help me to see myself the way You see me. Help me to see my purpose and value through Your eyes. I want to be a good success in Your sight and not that of the world. You are the only one that matters to me. I thank You, and I praise You in the matchless name of Jesus. Amen.

OUT OF THE BOX

SUCCESS IN YOUR CALLING COMES FROM FREEDOM IN CHRIST Jesus. You were never intended to be boxed in! Don't allow others to box you in or try to fit you into the wrong place because it makes them comfortable. As a mother of seven children, this frequently happened to me. Since I had so many children, I was automatically labeled Sunday School teacher, VBS leader, nursery director, childcare worker, etc. everywhere I went. I learned to stand up and speak out finally. I got tired of being boxed in and told I couldn't be or do anything else. I have so much more inside of me!

What have people tried to label you? What's really inside of you? You are a light made to shine. Don't dim that light to make others feel better, fit their convenience, or fit their preconceived notions. Shine! Get out of the box and stay there!

Success will require you to continually stretch and grow and remain outside of the box of your own understanding. Allow God to use you in such mighty ways that you can't comprehend and watch Him blow your mind! Don't try to fit in with or please the people of this world. The only one you have to please is God.

> Do not conform any longer to the pattern of this world,
> but be transformed by the renewing of your mind.
> Then you will be able to test and approve what God's
> will is-his good, pleasing and perfect will.

ROMANS 12:2 NIV

Don't be afraid to be different. You need to be who God called you to be, even if it means sticking out like a sore thumb because you refuse to go with the crowd. Dare to be different! God's got your back. He designed you to be different and set apart; following His ways instead of the ways of this world.

> But ye are a chosen generation, a royal priesthood,
> an holy nation, a peculiar people; that ye should shew
> forth the praises of him who hath called you
> out of the darkness into his marvelous light:

1 PETER 2:9 KJV

This particular verse says a lot about you (and me). I encourage you to memorize it to the best of your ability, engraving it in your mind, and writing it on your heart. It brings up points about yourself that are imperative for you to remember.

You are part of a chosen generation, set apart from the world, to be part of God's holy people. You are peculiar or in other words special, extraordinary, atypical, rare, and unique by design. Created to praise Him, you were called out of the darkness of this world and brought into His marvelous light.

You are set apart and special. You were never meant to fit in with this world, so stop trying to! By trying to fit in with this world, you are defeating His purpose. Be you! Be all that He's called you to be.

> I will praise thee; for I am fearfully
> and wonderfully made: marvelous are thy works;
> and that my soul knoweth right well.

PSALM 139:14 KJV

Praise God for who you are. Praise Him that you are different. Praise Him that you don't just fit in.

Father God, I thank You for creating me in Your own special way. I thank You that You haven't just made us all clones; that we are far from identical and that we are each unique and special in our own ways. Please help me to embrace my differences instead of trying to cover them up or fit in. I ask that You increase my boldness and that I won't be ashamed of my differences, but rather rejoice in them because they are a gift from You. In Jesus' name, amen.

COMFY WITH THE UNCOMFORTABLE

THE CHRISTIAN WALK WAS NEVER MEANT TO BE COMFORT-able. Was Jesus comfortable? As an infant, He had to lay in a bed of hay, that I'm sure had bugs in it, and was in a barn full of animals that stunk horrendously.

> And Jesus said to him, "Foxes have holes
> and birds of the air have nests, but the
> Son of Man has nowhere to lay His head."
>
> **LUKE 9:58 NKJV**

This scripture doesn't lead me to believe that Jesus' life was comfortable. His journey to the cross certainly wasn't comfortable. His death was the most agonizing possible and definitely not comfortable. Yet we as human beings, for some reason, are creatures of comfort. We tend to long for it, and even sacrifice for it. Many will sacrifice for comfort before they will sacrifice for Christ, some Christians included. People in that latter group need to re-evaluate their walk.

There are many verses in the Bible that point to the fact that we can't and shouldn't expect to be comfortable. In fact, many times we are told the opposite. Our joy is not to come from this world though, but rather from the Lord.

> So when Jesus heard these things, He said to him, "You still lack one thing. Sell all that you have and distribute to the poor, and you will have treasure in heaven; and come follow me." But when he heard this, he became very sorrowful, for he was very rich.

> **LUKE 18:22-23 NKJV**

Jesus was making it clear that He is supposed to be our main focus, our first priority. Clearly, when you are so attached to something that you can't give it up, it is proof that it is your first priority. The rich man was so focused on his belongings that he was unable to follow Christ. What is your focus? Are you able to truly follow Christ?

When you adopt your calling, it's best to get comfy with the uncomfortable. You will be stretched and required to grow. The Lord will ask or tell you to do things that are outside of your comfort zone or out of the box. Writing this book is one of those things for me. You will have to make sacrifices and learn to manage your time better. Your earthly obligations will not go away just because you've realized your Kingdom responsibilities.

I have told you all this so that you may have
peace in me. Here on earth you will have
many trials and sorrows. But take heart,
because I have overcome the world."

JOHN 16:33 NLT

This verse very plainly tells us that we will not have an easy
life. We are instructed to expect trouble so that we won't be
surprised by it. Look around you though, it's not as if worldly
troubles are limited to Christians. Expect to be uncomfortable.

Don't be surprised if friends and family walk away for a
time or even indefinitely. Increase your faith and courage,
even if just little by little, to live outside of the box of your
own comfort, the comfort of those around you, and people's
thoughts and expectations of you. No matter what you do,
follow the Lord's lead and don't rush ahead.

*Father God, please help me to maintain my focus on You. I
am humbling myself before You and acknowledging that You
are the Potter and I am the clay. Please help me to be more
yielded to Your will and Your stretching and reshaping of me.
I thank You for the process and the fact that You love me
enough to see me through to completion. Increase my faith
and courage to get out of the box and live outside of my comfort zone. I ask these things in the magnificent name of Jesus.
Amen.*

WEEKEND CHALLENGE

Studying

Study to shew thyself approved unto God,
a workman that needeth not to be ashamed,
rightly dividing the word of truth.

2 TIMOTHY 2:15 KJV

This weekend, spend some time studying spiritual gifts, beginning with the Bible. Every time you sit down to study pray and ask God to reveal to you that which He wants you to know and focus on right now. At the end of each study session thank Him for what you've learned and answered prayer. Begin your study by reading the following portions of the Bible: Romans, chapter 12; 1 Corinthians, chapters 12-14; and Ephesians, chapter 4. Once you have read these chapters, you may wish to read related commentaries, books specific to individual gifts, or books related to the spiritual gifts in general. Learn as much as you can, and then ask God what He wants you to do with this new knowledge.

Pray and Praise

Turn your worries into prayers, and praise Him in all circumstances! Get a piece of paper and write down every worry that you have right now. Write it like a checklist and leave room for notes next to every item. Now, pray about each item. Check it off the list once you've prayed about it, and next to it write: "Problem Solved–It Is Finished!" Remember, God has already worked it all out. He knows the beginning, middle, and the end.

When you are done praying over the things on your list, make a list of praises. You should have a lot now! Make sure you praise Him for all of the answered prayers. Let loose and praise in whatever way or ways you are led.

Peace with Your Piece

This challenge is more introspective. Do you know or have an idea of what your piece in the puzzle is? How do you feel about your piece? Are you growing to fully fill your position in the puzzle? Are there aspects of your piece in the puzzle that bother you or you struggle with? Have you moved into your slot?

Seriously think about these questions and any others you may have regarding your spot in the puzzle. You may find it helpful to do some research or talk to people who are doing similar things to what you are going to be doing. Most importantly, make it a focus of your prayer this weekend. Talk it over with God in detail. The goal is for you to have a greater sense of peace with your piece by the end of the weekend.

Be Unique

God doesn't expect us to live up to the expectations of others. We are only supposed to be living up to His expectations. That's not to say that we can be irresponsible and live however we please. It means that at times in our life people may have unrealistic or negative expectations of us, but that we are not to be concerned with them.

God made you to be a unique reflection of Himself in the earth. You have to be your unique self. After all, you can't be somebody else. That position is already taken. What are some of your quirks, features, habits, likes and dislikes that are less than common? What are some things about you that set you apart from others?

Maybe you're like me. I live in Texas, but I literally cannot drink tea. Anyone that's familiar with Texas and its natives knows that this is relatively unheard of! This is a cheesy example, but even small oddities like this one can have a purpose. For me, this one is a great conversation starter when used properly. You might have your own sense of style that makes you stand out in a crowd, but yet you look great. Perhaps you have a unique talent, skill, hobby, or interest.

Can you think of any way to capitalize on your one-of-a-kind aspects of who you are? For example, I use my dislike of tea to start conversations and potentially build valuable relationships. You may be able to use a rare talent to help others or provide an income for yourself or family. List the things that make up your unique self and write down any potential benefits or uses for these things. Finally, rejoice and thank God that you are different!

Another Stretch

This is another challenge to get you to think outside the box and stretch beyond your comfort zone. Think about the different people in your life that you see on a regular basis, but don't really know. This could be someone that works in the cubicle next to you, a person that always rides the same bus line as you, a person that works at a store or restaurant you frequent, or even someone that goes to your church but you just never get to talk to them. Think outside of the box and decide which of these people that came to mind would be the least likely to be a friend of yours. Pray and be sure that you've chosen the right person for this challenge.

Your challenge is to pray for this person all weekend. Ask God to open doors of opportunity for you to talk to them and get to know them better. Ask Him to help you build a relationship with this person that is within His will and divine purpose. Make a conscientious effort to start conversations with this person and be open to the possibility of it becoming a great friendship. The Lord may even lead you in sharing the gospel or your testimony with this person at some point.

Every person in your life, no matter how insignificant they may seem to you, is in your life for a reason, purpose, and season. Thank God for that person. Even the person that you think is too shy, weird, outgoing, or whatever other excuse you may have used to keep your distance, is in your life for a purpose. Their purpose in your life may not even be known to them, and it may be to challenge and grow you, serve you, teach you, make you think, or any other number of things.

Too often we limit ourselves by our boxed in thoughts and preconceived notions of people without even giving them a chance. Other times we just allow ourselves to be boxed into our comfort zones never wanting to come out or let others in. Stretch and see what God can do when you stop limiting the possibilities that are all around you!

A Great

PLEASURE

IN

LIFE

is Doing What
Others Say
You Can't

GREAT FAITH

Is anything too hard for the LORD?
I will return to you at the appointed time
next year and Sarah will have a son.

GENESIS 18:14 NIV

Abraham was a hundred years old when
his son Isaac was born to him. Sarah said,
"God has brought me laughter, and everyone
who hears about this will laugh with me."
And she added, "Who would have said to
Abraham that Sarah would nurse children?
Yet I have borne him a son in his old age."

GENESIS 21:5-7 NIV

EVEN THOUGH PEOPLE LIVING IN THAT ERA LIVED LONG LIVES,
it was still unheard of to have children at such an old
age. In our day and age, we would still view it the
same way. Sarah took pleasure in being part of something impossible. She did something that nobody
thought could ever happen.

Have you been given a dream or aspiration that no one else thought was possible? For me, writing a book was one of those many things, even though later in life people did come along and believe with me. Like many children, I was frequently told by other children and adults the things that I couldn't do, that I'd never amount to anything, and was never even told what I could do. But great faith does great things. When we have enough faith in God, it is easier to have faith that He will help us do the things He has called us to do. We know that He will help us if we step out in faith and persevere.

> Then Jesus answered,
> "Woman, you have great faith!
> Your request is granted."
> And her daughter was healed from that very hour.

MATTHEW 15:28 NIV

This woman had great faith in Jesus and His ability to heal her daughter. The disciples were trying to get Jesus to turn her away. I imagine that she saw this and realized what was happening. Her faith by this point was too great to quit. The woman's great faith caused her to persist until her daughter was healed.

As we move along toward a thing in faith, our faith actually increases. When we reach an obstacle that's when we should look back to see how far God has brought us and keep pushing forward towards that thing. You only need itty, bitty mustard seed faith to get started. Rely on the Lord to keep you going and to continually increase your faith. Keep your eyes open to what He is doing as you go and grow through the process.

> But Jesus looked at them and said,
> "With men it is impossible, but not with God;
> for with God all things are possible."

MARK 10:27 NKJV

> So Jesus said to them, "Because of your unbelief;
> for assuredly, I say to you, if you have faith as a
> mustard seed, you will say to this mountain,
> 'Move from here to there,' and it will move;
> and nothing will be impossible for you. However,
> this kind does not go out except by prayer and fasting."

MATTHEW 17:20-21 NKJV

Do you have mustard seed faith? Believe God for what you need and what He has put inside of you to do great things. Press forward and look back on the things that God has done for you so far! Without faith, it is impossible to please God. Remember, great faith does great things!

> And without faith it is impossible to please God because
> anyone who comes to him must believe that he exists
> and that he rewards those who earnestly seek him.

HEBREWS 11:6 NIV

Heavenly Father, thank You for the measure of faith You've given me. Please increase my faith and give me a clear vision of the great things You will for me to do with that faith. Block the negative thoughts and attacks of the enemy past, present, and future. Help me to only hear and heed Your thoughts towards me. I ask this in Jesus' mighty name. Amen.

FOLLOWING CHRIST

You shall walk in all the way that the LORD your
God has commanded you, that you may live,
and that it may go well with you, and that you
may live long in the land that you shall possess.

DEUTERONOMY 5:33 ESV

WHEN THE LORD GIVES ME SOMETHING SPECIFIC TO DO, I
frequently have naysayers. Sometimes I am required
to walk in opposition in order to be obedient, but at
the end of the day, the only person I truly have to
answer to is God.

Most of the time those that oppose what you're
doing can't comprehend or see the vision. They think
that it's too big or complicated. It usually is! Don't let
the enemy trick you into saying they are too simple
or to discourage you from doing that thing. Here's a
news flash for you, if God calls you to do something
that's bigger or more complicated than you can figure
out all on your own, it's a good sign that it really is
from God!

The question then becomes, what to do about it. You bathe it in prayer. Also, have anyone else that may support you pray for it. Let the Lord guide your steps, being careful not to lean on your own understanding.

Keep steady my steps according to your promise,
and let no iniquity get dominion over me.
PSALM 119:133 ESV

If we live by the Spirit, let us also keep
in step with the Spirit.
GALATIANS 5:25 ESV

Trust in the LORD with all your heart, and do not lean
on your own understanding. In all your ways acknowledge him, and he will make straight your paths.
PROVERBS 3:5-6 ESV

God wants all of us. You have to give him your all in order to follow Him. You can't hold back on areas of your life, and only allow Him access to bits and pieces.

Jesus said to him, "If you would be perfect, go, sell
what you possess and give to the poor, and you will
have treasure in heaven; and come, follow me.
MATTHEW 19:21 ESV

In this verse, Jesus is talking to the rich man. You too are rich. Your riches may not be regarding money, but you have time, talent, treasure, family, friends, etc. The Lord requires that you put Him first though; above all else. In everything you do, acknowledge Him.

> And whatever you do, in word or deed, do everything in the name of the Lord Jesus, giving thanks to God the Father through him.
>
> Colossians 3:17 ESV

Daddy God, show me how to completely surrender all to You. I want to follow You with my all, my everything, withholding nothing. I love You! I worship and adore You, and I long to please, serve, and follow You. Please show me any areas that I'm holding back in or blocking You out and help me to release them to You. I ask these things in the wonderful name of Jesus. Amen.

DISCIPLINE

THE PEOPLE THAT HAVE DONE SOME OF THE GREATEST THINGS in life all have one thing in common. That thing is discipline. Like everything else, we can look to Jesus for our example. The first things that come to mind are the fact that He was disciplined to fast and pray and resist the temptations of the devil.

But have nothing to do with worldly fables
fit only for old women. On the other hand,
discipline yourself for the purpose of godliness;
for bodily discipline is only of little profit,
but godliness is profitable for all things,
since it holds promise for the present life
and also for the life to come.

1 TIMOTHY 4:7-8 NASB

It takes great discipline and perseverance to do great things. You must guard your time and use it wisely, being careful to maintain focus. You have to be diligent in your work and not allow yourself to become idle or stagnant.

Now we command you, brothers in the name of
our Lord Jesus Christ, that you keep away from any
brother who is walking in idleness and not in accord
with the tradition that you received from us.

2 THESSALONIANS 3:6 ESV

Not only so, but we also glory in our sufferings,
because we know that suffering produces perseverance;
perseverance character; and character, hope.
And hope does not put us to shame, because God's
love has been poured out into our hearts through the
Holy Spirit, who has been given to us.

ROMANS 5:3-5 NIV

It can be difficult to go against the grain and work towards
your goal when people speak against it and tell you that you
can't do it. Many people often want a result, but aren't willing
to do the work; so, it's only natural that they will try to dis-
tract you from your work. You will have to do the things that
other people aren't willing to do in order to achieve results
that no one else has achieved or can. Yes, you will suffer, but
if you allow it, you will increase in perseverance, character,
and hope. This, along with the help of the Holy Spirit, will
make it possible to do things others say you can't. Do you
maintain your focus and manage your time well? Are you diligent and careful not to be still or get stuck?

Father God, You alone are worthy, holy, and almighty, and I long to fulfill the purposes You've placed in me. Please help me to endure and push forward towards the goal. Strengthen me to walk this thing out to completion. Increase my focus and discipline and keep me from idleness. In the name of Jesus, I pray. Amen.

JOY UNSPEAKABLE

MOSES PARTED THE RED SEA. ESTHER BECAME QUEEN AND saved her people. Lazarus came back to life after being dead for days. I'm sure there were people that thought these things were impossible, but with God all things are possible.

Sure, these are extreme examples, but they are great illustrations of people doing things that seemed impossible. Yours may not be as extreme, but you are destined for greatness. Maybe you'll be the first in your family to finish college, own a business, or hold a political office. These things are not less than, and you will encounter opposition. You will also experience unspeakable joy when you do what God created you to do despite the opposition.

> Consider it pure joy, my brothers and sisters,
> whenever you face trials of many kinds,
> because you know that the testing
> of your faith produces perseverance.

JAMES 1:2-3 NIV

Most of the awesome things you will do in life will take time. After all, Lazarus was dead for days and Esther had a lengthy process to go through just to become queen. The process can't be avoided, but it is definitely worth it in the end. A lot of people aren't willing to go through it, and therefore forfeit their dreams, calling, and greatness. Are you willing to be persistent and work, or are you going to forfeit your destiny?

You are greater than your greatest doubt or fear, and your God is the God of the impossible. The Lord loves to show His love to us in circumstances that the human mind views as impossible and can't fully comprehend. Our salvation, Jesus' life, death, and resurrection are perfect representations of this. What inconceivable things have you been called to do?

> May the God of hope fill you with all joy
> and peace as you trust in him, so that you may
> overflow with hope by the power of the Holy Spirit.

ROMANS 15:13 NIV

Our hope is in Christ. When we walk in our God-given assignments, we can rest assured that He is there, in control, and making the way. This is where our joy and peace come from. We know that our mission will be accomplished according to His will because we are walking in obedience. Our joy is visible, unspeakable and our peace is unexplainable. It can only be God, and gives us an incredible testimony!

Heavenly Father, You are awesome and perfect in all Your ways. You are my source of joy, peace, protection, and provision. I want to live a life that is full of abundant joy and peace and is an acceptable offering to You. Please make my purposes absolutely clear and obvious to me. Lead me and guide me and help me to not stray off course. I thank You and I praise You in the mighty name of Jesus, amen.

LEADERSHIP

BE A LEADER, A TRAILBLAZER, A TRENDSETTER IN YOUR OWN way. Frequently people will say that you can't do something because you stick out and don't fit into their box. As human beings, we have a bad habit of confining people according to our preconceived notions. What's worse is that we tend to limit God in the same way!

We were never all supposed to be the same. God makes each person unique and for specific reasons. We aren't clones. Why does everybody strive to fit in instead of standing out and being different for the Lord? There are many aspects and dimensions of God and we are supposed to be a reflection of Him in the earth. When we fail to be all He's called us to uniquely be and continue to grow more like Christ on a regular basis, we are robbing the world and those around us.

Be imitators of me, as I am of Christ

1 CORINTHIANS 11:1 ESV

We aren't supposed to be copying one another, except to the extent of being more like Jesus. As Christians, we are to be leaders; leading others to Christ. Instead, we've allowed ourselves to be influenced by the world around us. Many are swayed by society and succumb to political correctness. We can't sit around and wonder why there is so much injustice in the world. It's because many Christians have been asleep at the wheel and grown cold or apathetic.

> No soldier gets entangled in civilian pursuits,
> since his aim is to please the one who enlisted him.
> An athlete is not crowned unless
> he competes according to the rules.

2 TIMOTHY 2:4-5 ESV

This is a very real war or race. But what are our rules? How are we to contend for our heavenly crown? Of course, this is not everything, but here are a few directions for running our race:

> I press on toward the goal for the prize
> of the upward call of God in Christ Jesus.

PHILIPPIANS 3:14 ESV

> Do you not know that in a race all runners run,
> but only one receives the prize? So run that you
> may obtain it. Every athlete exercises
> self-control in all things. They do it to receive
> a perishable wreath, but we an imperishable.

1 CORINTHIANS 9:24-25 ESV

If you were of the world, the world would love you as its own; but because you are not of the world, but I chose you out of the world, therefore the world hates you.

JOHN 15:19 ESV

We are called to press toward the goal. Run your race to win, and be a leader of the pack! Our prize is eternal life. You are chosen out of the world; not called to blend in. The church at large needs to wake up and get to work. Will you be the one to lead the way?

Father, Lord of heaven and earth, help me to be a true leader for You. Allow me to lead those around me in such a way that others are encouraged, drawn to You, and motivated to live up to their full potential to change the world. Grace me with Your strength, wisdom, knowledge, discernment, and endurance. Help me to fully understand my assignments here on earth and to complete them in excellence. I ask this in Jesus' name. Amen.

WEEKEND CHALLENGE

A Focused Fast

What is your great thing? This weekend your challenge is to focus on your great thing through fasting and prayer. There are many different kinds of fasts, and it really doesn't matter which kind you do. Fasts vary from complete fasts (meaning no food or drink for the duration of the fast) to fasting from only one thing, such as fried food and everything in between. Allow the Lord to lead you in the type of fast that would be best for you concerning your health, faith, and sacrifice required.

Remember that it's not about the fast, but rather your focus and behavior during it. Focus on Christ and pray for that great, impossible thing that He has called you to do. Pray for a divine strategy to accomplish that thing. Pray for increased faith and to get to the point that turning back is no longer an option. Your scripture focus for the weekend is Matthew 17.

Who to Follow

How do you follow Christ? What does that even look like? Who or what do you really follow?

Many people follow others on social media, the news, or the stock market. These are just a few examples. They often start and end their days by checking in on the thing or person they are following. Some even do it more frequently by checking in at lunch or periodically throughout the day.

Your challenge for the weekend is to truly put God first in all you do. Get up early, and before doing anything else pray, worship, and read your Bible. Do you generally check on the news or social media at lunch time or other times throughout your day? Well, if you do, skip it this weekend and check in with the Lord instead. Ask for direction and guidance for the rest of your day and thank Him for your day thus far. Before turning in for the night, check in with Him again. It is my prayer that you will allow this to become a regular habit for you.

Don't Idle

When a car sits and idles it is wasting gas. It's no different with us. When we are sitting still and not progressing towards those things the Lord has called us to, we are wasting precious time in idle. Purpose to press toward your goals and not be stagnant.

Focus your weekend on getting out of any ruts or bad habits you may have developed. Take specific steps to move toward and achieve your goals. Spend extra time with the Lord as well as any people you may have a relationship with that has grown a bit stagnant. Strengthen those relationships this weekend and refuse to be stagnant. It may sound like a lot, but overall you just need to make sure that you are making progress instead of sitting still. Allow the Holy Spirit to guide you in how to do this.

What's Your Impossible

We all have something that we are called to do that we or others around us believe to be impossible. Do you know what your impossible is? Spend your weekend learning about it. Are there examples or similar situations in the Bible? If so, start there.

Do some research. Go online and read articles, look at pictures, and watch videos. Learn more about what it is that you are called to do or become. Develop a game plan on how to follow through. Reach out to anyone you may know that is already doing that thing or that can help you with it. Perhaps you've already done these things and have begun your journey if so, spend some time making strides on that journey this weekend. Allow God to show Himself in your life by making the impossible, possible!

Lead the Pack

Are you a leader or a follower? Who do you lead? Don't get me wrong; there isn't anything wrong with being a follower in certain situations. We are all supposed to be following Christ and on our jobs, we have to follow our boss. In life overall though, as believers, we are supposed to be leaders and set the standard.

We can lead on our jobs even if we aren't in a leadership position. We do this by maintaining a standard of excellence and integrity in our work performance as well as our relationships with bosses and co-workers. We also lead in our communities and churches by our examples in what we do, how we react, and how we treat others.

You don't have to be a titled leader to be in leadership. God titles you. Man just confirms what God has said about you. Being a leader means living a life of integrity and maintaining a standard of excellence right where you are. Even stay at home moms or dads are leaders, and probably the most important leaders at that! They are leading the next generation and determining our future by how they lead their children.

Look at your life and where you spend the majority of your time. Is it in your workplace, home, church, or community? Are you leading in excellence or just following the crowd? Evaluate your areas of influence and your leadership roles. Ask God to help you lead in the places and capacities that He has placed you. Petition Him to help you in all areas that you may be lacking. Be a leader and not just a follower. When you are in a position of following, do it in excellence. Be a leader in your following!

DON'T

LET

THE PAST

and
Useless Details
Choke Your
Existence

FORGIVENESS

Let all bitterness and indignation and wrath
(passion, rage, bad temper) and resentment
(anger, animosity) and quarreling (brawling,
clamor, contention) and slander (evil-speaking,
abusive or blasphemous language) be banished
from you, with all malice (spite, ill will,
or baseness of any kind). And become useful
and helpful and kind to one another,
tenderhearted (compassionate, understanding,
loving-hearted) forgiving one another
(readily and freely) as God in Christ forgave you.

EPHESIANS 4:31-32 AMP

THIS PORTION OF SCRIPTURE COMMANDS US TO FORGIVE AS
Christ forgave us. Why are all the other things mentioned, i.e. rage, anger, and bitterness? It's because these things often are a result of unforgiveness. We are also instructed to banish or get rid of these things in us and become useful.

Now, wait a minute! Why does it say we are to become useful? Well, that's because unforgiveness and the various results of it can serve as bondage in our lives. When we don't forgive, we tend to get frozen or stuck in the past. By doing this, we allow our past (and often useless details) to choke our existence. We can't move forward because we're stuck in our past!

Do you think someone has done something to you that's unforgivable? I do not doubt your pain or the impact the wrong had on you, but none of us are perfect. Sin is sin, and we all fall short of the glory of God. As born again believers, whether a liar or a murderer, we are forgiven. There isn't a sin in God's eyes that doesn't need to be forgiven. Likewise, there's none too great that He can't forgive because He is God. We are called to forgive the way He did.

In Psalm 51, David goes to the Lord with a repentant heart, seeking forgiveness. He had been slacking off, coveting, stole another man's wife, and then had that man killed in battle! Yet David was a man after God's own heart. He said the things in Psalm 51 in faith, with conviction and repentance in his heart knowing that God would forgive him.

In 2 Chronicles 33, Manasseh was downright evil and defiant. He did things God hated, but He still forgave him. So, can you say that anything that you've done or anything that someone else has done to you can't be forgiven? In Judges 15 and 16 we see that Samson had a belief similar to today's world views of revenge and getting even and it was a vicious back and forth cycle. Lack of forgiveness breeds anger, revenge, contempt, and is the root of bitterness.

Unforgiveness becomes bondage and slavery if you don't address it quickly. I say that because it clouds your vision and you lose your focus. Your perspective changes, and you can become bitter and enraged. You focus on the wrong, your personal sufferings, and the person that wronged you. You may even get mad that they aren't suffering like you. Part of the reason for this is because it's like you're drinking poison!

You become so focused on the situation that you can't see straight. You've likely disconnected from God. When all you focus on is a problem or issue, it becomes magnified and you've made God tiny in your sight. What's more, is that the person that wronged you is typically oblivious and not suffering. Unforgiveness is like drinking a poison and expecting the other person to die.

Forgiveness isn't for the person you're forgiving. It's for you! By forgiving quickly, you avoid being in bondage. Once you're already in that bondage, the only way out is through forgiveness.

Forgiveness is a choice. You first need to choose to forgive the person. It probably won't be easy (especially if you've been holding onto unforgiveness for awhile). Pray and ask God for help to forgive as He has forgiven you. Ask Him to help you let go of the offense or offenses and to stop playing out the scenario in your head over and over again. Last, but certainly not least, pray for that person. As a word of caution, if you find yourself praying for punishment for that person, you haven't truly forgiven them. You need to go back to the Lord with a sincere heart and ask for help in forgiving as you have been forgiven.

Dear Heavenly Father, I come to You asking for Your help. You alone are almighty, all knowing, and all powerful. You alone can help me with this. I thank you for forgiving me of all my sins. Please teach me how to forgive like You, quickly and completely. Help me to not be easily offended, and to love like You do. I ask this in the mighty and glorious name of Jesus. Amen.

DISCERNMENT

Do not judge by appearances,
but judge with right judgment.

JOHN 7:24 ESV

WHEN IT COMES TO YOUR PAST, WHAT DO YOU DO WITH IT?
Do you judge rightly which things to hold on to and
what things to let go of? We all have memories and a
past. Some memories are pleasant, others are not, and
some are even painful.

What we go through in life is what shapes us and
makes us into the person we are today, as well as the
person we are to become. Sometimes we even go
through things for the benefit of someone else,
because it's the ministry God has called us to. That
can be a shocker for some; I know! The key lies in
being able to discern what's what.

The truth is there are no accidents or coincidences
when it comes to God. Everything happens for a reason and a purpose. Every member of your family was

intentionally handpicked by God Himself, whether you can stand them or not! Nothing surprises God.

> For we are his workmanship, created in Christ Jesus
> for good works, which God prepared beforehand,
> that we should walk in them.

EPHESIANS 2:10 ESV

God has prepared good works for you and me, and it doesn't matter what we've been through. Do you think that something in your past disqualifies you from serving, being able to do good works, or living a good life? Even the worst things you've done or that have been done to you have a purpose. The question is whether you rightly judge them or not. Life is a matter of perspective, or how you look at things.

Try to take a few minutes now and look at your past through God's eyes. Go ahead and do it now. I'll wait. When we look back at our life through His eyes, we should be able to see how He brought us out of bad situations, things that were bad that He turned for our good, and things that we learned due to things we did or experienced.

Were you able to see things in your past through the Lord's eyes and how all things work together, or do you just see good and bad? When you can see your life through the clear lens of God, you can see His handiwork. If you weren't able to see past a negative situation in your life and how He has used it or fixed it, please go back and look at it again. Look at it prayerfully, as many times as necessary, asking God to reveal the positives to you. Now go back and look at the positives such as any lessons learned, relationships formed, and experience gained. Keep in mind that it may not have been for you, but for the benefit of someone else.

When we choose to hold on to things from our past in an improper context, it can hold us back and choke and smother us. Yes, we all go through terrible things in life, and it hurts us. That's not the end of our story though. I grew up in poverty compared to others around me. This could have caused a lot of negatives such as a "woe is me" complex, bitterness, or a sense of entitlement. Instead, I've learned to be thrifty and resourceful, appreciate what I have, and have compassion for those with less than me at any given time.

Don't let your past hold you back from your future because you aren't looking at it through the proper lens. Make a conscientious decision to look at your past, present, and future through God's eyes. Ask Him to reveal things that you may have missed.

Father God, I come humbly before You in awe, adoration, and amazement of all the things You have done in me, for me, through me, and the things that You have brought me out of. I truly want to see things the way You see them. Please help me to see myself, my circumstances, and my past, present, and future the way You see them. In Jesus' name, I pray, amen.

TIME TO MOVE

I don't mean to say that I've already achieved
these things or that I have already achieved
perfection. But I press on to possess that
perfection for which Christ Jesus first possessed
me. No dear brothers and sisters I have not
achieved it, but I focus on this one thing:
forgetting the past and looking forward to what
lies ahead, I press on to reach the end of the
race and receive the heavenly prize for which
God, through Christ Jesus, is calling us.

PHILIPPIANS 3:12-14 NLT

PAUL DIDN'T HAVE A PRETTY PAST! HE WASN'T ABOUT TO LET
that stop him though. He knew there was much more
ahead of him and that dwelling on his past would
only hinder him from his future. Is there anything
holding you back?

We can't expect to drive forward or get anywhere if
we are constantly looking in the rearview mirror! We
must focus straight ahead and continue on. Sure, our
past is full of useless details, but some are also useful.

When it comes to dealing with our past, we can't look at it with wishful thinking. We can't go back and change it. We aren't supposed to be stuck in it like glue. However, there are lessons learned, and that is what we need to carry into our future. Paul was an unsavory character before he became Paul. Through his past, he learned how not to behave. What have you learned from your past that can or has helped you in your present and can help in your future?

Paul knew that there was much more in store for him. It wasn't just this life that he was looking at either. He was looking at his heavenly reward and spending eternity with Christ. What are you looking at? What's your focus?

When our focus is on the past, we tend to start going in reverse. We live in the past instead of the present, repeating past mistakes and habits and staying in prior and faulty mindsets. Are you living in your past or present? Today is a gift; that's why it's called the present, and your past has already passed. So, let your past pass you by right now as you vow to stop staring in your rearview mirror. Let's be like Paul. Shift the gears in your mind to drive, and press that gas pedal to move on to your future. It's time to move!

Lord, help me to move forward only holding on to the lessons You've taught me and those things that You've given me to better me. Please reveal a glimpse of the potential You've placed in me, and the future I may have. Please help me to move and press towards the end of the race. I know my strength and help come from You and that's why I ask You in Jesus' name. Amen.

FACE FORWARD

But Jesus told him, "Anyone who puts a hand
to the plow and then looks back
is not fit for the Kingdom of God."

LUKE 9:62 NLT

IN THIS SECTION OF SCRIPTURE, JESUS WAS TEACHING ABOUT the cost of following Him. He had just told one man to let the spiritually dead bury their own and go preach the Gospel. Luke 9:62 was His response to someone that wanted to go back and say goodbye to their family.

The Lord wants all of us, not just bits and pieces. We aren't supposed to hold on to our past or anything of this life. We need to face forward and look ahead to what God is calling us to instead of complaining, whining, or moaning about things that happened in the past.

Remember ye not the former things, neither consider
the things of old. Behold, I will do a new thing;
now it shall spring forth; shall ye not know it? I will even
make a way in the wilderness, and rivers in the desert.

ISAIAH 43:18-19 KJV

Do you want to see new things that the Lord is doing in, through, and around you? You have to wake up, open your eyes, face forward, and stop looking back! I don't know about you, but I want to see the new and be fit for the Kingdom of God.

We need to understand and realize that if we are born-again Christians, we have the Holy Spirit within us and are new creatures in Christ.

Therefore if any man be in Christ, he is a new creature:
old things are passed away;
behold, all things are become new.

2 CORINTHIANS 5:17 KJV

Sometimes we hold on to pieces of our past that are filled with shame or regret. We cannot change the past. There's no need or purpose in hanging on to shame or regret from past sins. As a believer, you are forgiven and new. The Lord does not see you as your past sin, even if you or others do. Let me tell you something; it doesn't matter how others see you or what they think about you. What matters is the condition of your heart and how the Lord sees you. You are not the sum total of your past mistakes. Please remember, you are a forgiven and new creature. Is there anything that you are holding on to?

On a piece of paper write down those things that you haven't let go of. Tell the Lord that you are trusting Him to help you release these things to face and move forward with Him. Now rip up that paper into teeny tiny pieces and throw them away.

Heavenly Father, I thank You that I am forgiven and set free from the bondage of my past by the blood of Jesus. I thank You that I am a new creature in You. Please help me to keep my face forward and to move forward with You to become who You've destined me to be and fulfill the purpose You have placed inside of me. I thank You, and I praise You in the matchless name of Jesus, my Lord, and Savior. Amen.

LOOK TO THE HEAVENS

Lift up your eyes and look to the heavens:
Who created all these? He who brings out the
starry host one by one and calls them each by
name. Because of his great power and mighty
strength, not one of them is missing.

ISAIAH 40:26 NIV

I lift up my eyes to the hills–where does my help
come from? My help comes from the LORD
the Maker of heaven and earth.

PSALM 121:1-2 NIV

LOOK UP! LOOK TO THE HEAVENS, LOOK TO THE LORD WHO
created and protects you. An issue we may all face
from time to time is a wrong focus. We need to keep
our focus on God.

The world is full of pasts. You have your personal
past just as every other person does. Then you have
the collective pasts of families, cities, nations, etc.

There are useless details all around us. Things that really wouldn't matter or amount to a hill of beans if we were to die tomorrow. Yet, we often make the mistake of getting caught up in these things.

Our world is full of chaos and distractions. The enemy uses this to take our focus away from Christ. We get caught up in our own little worlds or problems. We may even get caught up in the problems of the world in such a way that we become overwhelmed to the point that we freeze up. Because our focus is wrong and we are overwhelmed we forget about the God of the universe. We forget about the things we can do to bring about change; so we do nothing! This is exactly what the enemy wants.

Some may lose their faith. Many become cynical and hopeless and have a hardened heart. For some, their hearts are hardened to other people and the Lord.

When we don't look to God for help and hope, we lose our effectiveness because we are doing things in our own strength. Our strength and help come from the Lord. We can't forget this. When we do, we forget the power of prayer, and so we end up not praying at all! We forget that He can help us, and so we do nothing at all about the situations that overwhelm us. When really, in fact, there are often things we can do, whether large or small, that could improve or change the matter at hand. Instead, we become too lazy or apathetic.

Father God, I love You, and I want to serve and please You. Please help me to keep my focus on You. Help me to see the power I have in You to affect change in situations and to remember that in all things I need to pray. Help me to pray without ceasing. I ask these things in Jesus' mighty name. Amen.

WEEKEND CHALLENGE

Pray for Your Enemies

I know that this is counterintuitive, but Jesus instructed us to pray for our enemies. That doesn't mean that we should pray for their demise! We can pray for the Lord to soften their heart and draw them unto Him, but we can't pray for Him to punish them. That wouldn't be a proper prayer with a pure heart. Pray that God will place godly people around them, or if you're super bold, pray that He will use you to draw them to Christ.

Do you have someone you need to forgive today? Do you have someone you've recently forgiven or a person that you see as an enemy? Write out a prayer for that person or people. Evaluate it and see if you've created it with pure motives; if so, pray this prayer throughout your weekend. Watch God begin to soften your heart towards the person.

Clear Lens

A part of discernment is being able to evaluate and know a person's motives. It's the same with situations. We need to be able to determine rightly if some of the things we are involved in should be a part of our lives or not. This is not to say that a person or situation should just be discarded. It's possible that some circumstances need to be tweaked.

Here's an example. Let's say that you have a group of friends that you go to a bar with once or twice a month on Saturday nights. The result is that you spend too much money and stay out too late. This causes you to miss church and not have tithes or money to pay all of your bills. This doesn't necessarily mean that you shouldn't have anything to do with these friends. It means that you shouldn't be hanging out at a bar with them on a Saturday night. Perhaps you just need to go to a restaurant or invite them to your place. After all, you may be their only exposure to Christ.

Now, I know that was a pretty intense and controversial example, but I wanted to work with something clear and understandable. Your challenge now is to take a deep look at your life, relationships, and activities. Do you have anything that needs adjusting or you need to be rid of? Make a game plan to do this and actually follow through with it.

Do you need more of a challenge? Is there a relationship or activity that would enhance your Christian walk or enable you to serve better in the Kingdom? Make an action plan to nurture and grow that relationship or activity and do it!

Goals to Go

Have you ever set goals before? Some people have a great habit of making goals and going after them. Some people make them and forget them, and still, some don't even bother while others just don't know how. Think of goals as your destinations or stops in life. The plans or steps to achieve those goals is your map or GPS.

It's just like when you're driving a car; without a goal or destination, you don't know where you're going. Would you just get in your car and drive with no purpose or destination? Well, your life is the same way. Without goals, you don't know where you're going, and you're just driving through life. To get somewhere, you must know where you are going. You also need this so that you know when you've arrived. Goals do have a purpose and function.

Take some time to prayerfully consider your goals, where you want to go in life. If setting goals is something new for you start off small by setting goals for next week, next month, and three months from now. Don't forget to write them down so you can look back on them, don't forget them, and know when you've achieved them. Once you've mastered this, you're ready to move on to the next stage and write goals for 3, 6, and 12 months. You can always move up. I know some people that write goals for 5 and 10 years. To be perfectly honest, I'm not there yet!

Once you've written your goals out, write an action plan. Think of the step-by-step process. For some people thinking from the beginning or where they are now, and following a natural progression works best for them. Here's something that may mess with your head though. I know it did mine when I heard it! Try starting from the end and working your way backward. This method actually helps you to visualize a thing better, and once you can see yourself achieving your goal and the steps required, you are more likely to follow through. Write your vision, make it plain, and take action.

Personal Growth

It has been my personal experience in my walk with the Lord that as I get over one sin or issue, another one comes to light. That's not to say that it's something new. It's been there all along, but in the last season I finally conquered a particular issue, and now God is working on another one in me. It's existed all along, but it wasn't the one He wanted me to focus on in that season.

Maybe you've noticed this in your life. Have you ever gotten frustrated when you conquered something and then realized that you had a new issue to focus on? The Lord doesn't try to beat you up or make you feel bad. He's trying to grow you up and mature you. Growth requires stretching, change, and yes, sometimes even pain.

Reflect back on your life. Are you able to see areas in which you've grown? What does He have you working on or addressing now? Prayerfully consider some things that you can do to address the current issue that is your focus. Choose one of these things and start doing it right now. You are an overcomer!

Work of His Hands

Sometimes we all need a change of scenery, and sometimes we need to change the way we look at things. Your challenge is to do just that! Try spending some time with your Heavenly Father in a new place and look at things in a new way. If you frequently pray at your kitchen table try going outdoors. Sit under a tree if you usually sit on the porch. Just like a good marriage or other relationships, sometimes you need to spice things up. Why should our relationship with God be any different?

Look to the heavens. Look at all the things God has created for your good pleasure, such as the sun, moon, sky, trees, stars, etc. Listen to the birds sing and the sounds of His creation all around you. When was the last time you truly appreciated a sunrise or sunset? Your challenge is to make the time to do that now.

When we marvel at all the amazing things God has created and done for us, we tend to remember who He is. The same God that created the universe created you and loves you too. He's able to do whatever you need of Him. As you wonder at the work of His hands, remember that He is able. Take the limits off of what He can do for you.

You Cannot
Love Life Until You

LIVE

THE

LIFE

You Love

CREATED

IN ORDER TO LIVE THE LIFE YOU LOVE, YOU HAVE TO KNOW who you are. You need a firm grasp on your identity and where you've come from. You are created and blessed!

> So God created man in His own image;
> He created him in the image of God;
> He created them male and female.

GENESIS 1:27 HCSB

> He created them male and female.
> When they were created,
> He blessed them and called them man.

GENESIS 5:2 HCSB

You are created in the image of God! God thinks so much of you that He made you in His image; not like anything else. You weren't just sloppily thrown together. You're not some freak of evolution that started as a fish or ape. More importantly, despite what anyone else may have said or told you, you are not a mistake or accident! You were created on purpose, full of purpose, and for a purpose. Even more than that, you are blessed!

> I will praise You, because I have been remarkably
> and wonderfully made. Your works are wonderful,
> and I know this very well. My bones were not hidden
> from You when I was made in secret, when I was
> formed in the depths of the earth. Your eyes saw me
> when I was formless; all my days were written in Your
> book and planned before a single one of them began.

PSALM 139:14-16 HCSB

Did you catch that? You are remarkable! God knows the very depths and core of your being. Nothing is secret or a surprise to Him. You and all the days of your life were planned before you were even born. You can rest assured that no matter how hard your life may be, it is exactly as it is supposed to be, it was pre-planned, and all for God's glory.

> For we are His creation-created in Christ Jesus
> for good works, which God prepared ahead
> of time so that we should walk in them.

EPHESIANS 2:10 HCSB

You were created for good works. God had a plan for you before you were ever born. Often, God wants even better for us than we can even want for ourselves. How many times have you prayed for something and God answered differently than you expected, but it also turned out way better than what you could have even imagined?

We need to understand that we are blessed and intentionally and intimately created for God's glory. We are created in His image for His purpose. You are full of purpose, and God has great things in store for you if you will allow Him to work in you and through you.

Heavenly Father of all creation, I thank You, and I praise You for creating me. Thank You for filling me with purpose and for the good things that You have in store for me. I thank You for creating me in Your image, and I ask that You help me to do those good works and fulfill my purposes in life. I ask that You help me to live a life that is pleasing to You and brings You glory. In Christ Jesus, I pray. Amen.

BE YOU

IN A WORLD WHERE EVERYONE IS EITHER VYING FOR POSI-
tions or trying to copy everyone else, life can be pretty
tough. To truly love your life to any extent, you need
to know who you are and be yourself. I'm not talking
about the world's version, where everybody is "keeping it real" and saying that it's ok to sin because it's just
who they are. I'm saying to be who you are in Christ.

> But ye are a chosen generation,
> a royal priesthood, an holy nation,
> a peculiar people; that ye should shew forth
> the praises of him who hath called you
> out of darkness into his marvelous light:
>
> **1 PETER 2:9 KJV**

You are peculiar or strange, different. You aren't of the
world. You're not supposed to blend in or be like
everyone else. You're supposed to stand out and be
different. You are His marvelous light in the darkness.
He created you to shine, so embrace your peculiarity
and be you. Don't try to be like the world.

Yet LORD, You are our Father;
we are the clay, and You are our potter;
we all are the work of Your hands.

ISAIAH 64:8 HCSB

Let your Father mold you and make you into the person He created you to be. He's not finished with you yet. Don't resist Him by trying to conform to this world, and don't be a square peg shoved into a round hole. Be all that He's created you to be!

Did not the One who made me in the womb
also make them? Did not the same God form
us both in the womb?

JOB 31:15 HCSB

God makes it known that we are all created equal. That doesn't mean that we are all the same though. We can respect each other's differences without trying to be the same. Yes, God will put people in your life to influence and mentor you as part of your shaping and growing process. Even though there are things that you are supposed to glean from other godly people, you are not to become a carbon copy of them. Do you, because you are the best you, and nobody else can do it!

I promise you that each person on this planet has both good and bad traits, even if you can't see them. Most people with mentors are focused on one or two things and tend to not see or they overlook faults in their mentor. I think the Lord intends it to be this way so that we can learn from them what we are supposed to. It's never a good idea to try to become an exact replica of them though. You have to be yourself while allowing godly people to pour into you. Allow God to work on ridding you of some bad traits while improving the good ones. Become all that God intends you to be, and most importantly, be you!

Father God, thank You for making me who I am. Please give me the courage and boldness to be all that You intend me to be. Help me to stand out and shine for You. I humbly submit to Your molding and making me into all You desire me to be. Please help me to resist the urge just to blend in and be like everyone else. I ask these things in the matchless name of Jesus. Amen.

LIVE

IN ORDER TO LOVE LIFE, YOU HAVE TO LIVE. WHAT EXACTLY does that mean though? Some people think of living it up socially, partying, or even being reckless. When I say "live," I'm using God's standards; not man's. As Christians, the life we love should be the life Christ has called us to. When we truly love Him, that's how we want to live anyway. Please understand that once we fully embrace and begin to live the life He has called us to, we will love life because we are being obedient, not that we love it and don't want to lose it. There's a difference.

Be very careful, then, how you live-not as unwise but as wise, making the most of every opportunity, because the days are evil.

EPHESIANS 5:15-16 NIV

We need to be wise with our lives. They are limited and an example to others. Our wisdom cannot be worldly wisdom though. It needs to be godly wisdom. How do we get godly wisdom?

But if any of you lacks wisdom, let him ask of God,
who gives to all generously and without reproach,
and it will be given to him.

JAMES 1:5 NASB

And do not be conformed to this world,
but be transformed by the renewing of your mind,
so that you may prove what the will of God is,
that which is good and acceptable and perfect.

ROMANS 12:2 NASB

We aren't to be like the world so we can't always be living according to worldly wisdom. When we renew our minds by reading our Bible, we learn what God's will is. It is then our responsibility to put what we learn into action. By doing this, we are obedient to Christ, an example to others, and we prove or show God's will through our example.

In that, I command you today to love the LORD
your God, to walk in His ways and to keep
His commandments and His statutes and
His judgments, that you may live and multiply,
and that the LORD your God may bless you
in the land where you are entering to possess it.

DEUTERONOMY 30:16 NASB

Notice the command is today, not tomorrow or a year from now or ten years from now, but today. We aren't supposed to party today and then live holy later when we finally decide to. We aren't promised next year, next month, next week, tomorrow, or even our next breath!

The life we love should be the life that Christ has called us to. When we truly surrender to Him, we desire nothing more than to serve, honor, and please Him. Are you living as God intended? I'm not asking if you're perfect, but rather that you are making steady progress and continually seeking more of Him. Daily improvements and doing your ultimate best should be the norm for you.

Heavenly Father, I realize that this life is not my own. The life You've given me is a gift, blessing, and responsibility. You alone can make my path straight. Please help me to love life by living a life that is pleasing and acceptable to You. Help me to love You and others more. Pour into me Your wisdom and knowledge that I can make right decisions in my life. In the precious name of Jesus, I pray, amen.

INTENTIONAL

ARE YOU LIVING ON PURPOSE OR DOES IT SEEM AS IF LIFE IS just carrying you away? We need to be intentional with our life. Make it a point to learn, grow, love, and live like Jesus. When we just allow life to drag us along we can't expect to love life if we live contrary to Christ.

> Therefore be careful how you walk, not as unwise men but as wise, making the most of your time, because the days are evil. So then do not be foolish, but understand what the will of the Lord is. And do not get drunk with wine, for that is dissipation, but be filled with the Spirit,

EPHESIANS 5:15-18 NASB

You need to guard and value your time being fully aware and intentional in how you spend it. Once time is lost, you can't get it back. Personally, I think the enemy has a great weapon in technology. Television shows, video games, and social media have been proven to just suck up a lot of people's time and takes their time with the Lord and each other. Families have been destroyed because of it.

When you are deliberate with your time and allow the Holy Spirit to guide you, you'll be surprised by how much you can accomplish. Make an effort to learn to maximize your time. No excuses! What is it that the Lord has put on your heart that you don't think you have time for? Break it down into stages and get started on it. Pray about it, and God will give you a strategy to make the time to do it. Reclaim your time and life from the world! You have a purpose in this life!

> For if you remain silent at this time,
> relief and deliverance for the Jews will arise
> from another place, but you and your father's family
> will perish. And who knows but that you have
> come to a royal position for such a time as this?"

ESTHER 4:14 NIV

You may be thinking that this was only said for Esther. I need to challenge your thinking. You were born for such a time as this! You are royalty! Your heavenly Father is the King of Kings, and that makes you a prince if you're a male and a princess if you're a female! Someone needs what God has placed inside of you. Make a conscious decision to tame your time and do whatever He has called you to do.

Daddy God, I come to You knowing that You are the ultimate Father. I know that You have good plans for me and You give good gifts. So, Lord, I am asking for clarity in knowing what You've called me to do, and divine strategy to do those things and better manage my time. I trust You and believe You. I receive what You have for me today and every day, in Jesus' name. Amen.

FULLNESS OF JOY

You will make known to me the path of life;
In Your presence is fullness of joy;
In Your right hand there are pleasures forever.

PSALM 16:11 NASB

WHEN YOU HAVE THE FULLNESS OF JOY THAT COMES FROM
the Lord, you love life because you realize that you are
on assignment and that there is more than this life.

Now may the God of hope fill you with all joy
and peace in believing, so that you will abound
in hope by the power of the Holy Spirit.

ROMANS 15:13 NASB

Your joy and peace are attached to your believing and
provide hope. You can have hope that this too shall
pass. Have hope that God is still in control even
amidst the chaos in this world and that you will one
day spend eternity with Him.

As contradictory as it may seem, you can and
should have joy no matter what circumstances you

find yourself in. Your joy doesn't have to come from this world or this life. Your joy comes from the Lord. Here is an example that He has given us, of how we should behave in rough times and what can happen.

But about midnight Paul and Silas were praying and singing hymns of praise to God, and the prisoners were listening to them; and suddenly there came a great earthquake, so that the foundations of the prison house were shaken; and immediately all the doors were opened and everyone's chains were unfastened.

ACTS 16:25-26 NASB

This is a perfect example of how we should behave! They praised the Lord even when they were in prison. We should be praising Him in all circumstances. When we praise in times of trial and tribulation, we are inviting miracles and witnessing to others. Paul and Silas were setting an example for those around them.

I'm pretty sure that at the time they were praising, they probably would have preferred to be elsewhere but they knew that eventually, they would be with Jesus again. From that knowledge, they drew hope and joy and praised in the midst of their situation. God worked miracles for them that night! They were freed from bondage, but they didn't run. They remained as an example for the other prisoners, who were probably in some state of shock, and also remained. The fact that the prisoners stayed put is a miracle of sorts as well. Of course, the greatest miracle is that of the prison guard and his family. They were saved as a result of the whole thing.

"Nevertheless do not rejoice in this,
that the spirits are subject to you,
but rejoice that your names are recorded in heaven."

LUKE 10:20 NASB

You can rejoice that as a born-again believer, you are going to heaven! No matter what situation you are in right now, it isn't the end! You have an eternal life waiting for you and that is reason enough for you to have joy.

Heavenly Father, I praise You and I thank You for the gift of eternal life with You. I ask that You help me to praise You through all circumstances. Keep me focused on You so that my joy may be full and unwavering. Help me to be an example to others and draw them to You. In Jesus' name, amen.

WEEKEND CHALLENGE

Created Declarations

A declaration is a statement about a fact that you say in and with authority. An example could be, "God created me and He loves me." Your challenge for this week's ending is to create some declarations about yourself based on God's Holy Word and what He says about you. After you've written these down, say them out loud to yourself. You can do this in front of a mirror if you'd like or point to yourself for emphasis. The purpose in this is to get you to realize and focus on how God sees you, instead of how the world may see you.

A wonderful way to get started would be to look up some things like creation, provision, love, and man in the concordance of your Bible. Many Bibles have them in the back and it works similar to a dictionary. The words are in alphabetical order and point you to scriptures dealing with or containing that word. Something else that may help is to go back and read the devotion from this week that is subtitled "Created." Start each declaration with "I am..." There are some examples listed below.

- I am fearfully and wonderfully made.
- I am a child of the Most High God.
- I am valuable.

Mentor Search

Some people believe that once they grow up, they no longer have need of teachers. I disagree. You can have teachers at all stages of life and for various things. A mentor may be for your job, your Christian walk, how to get through a particular season or situation in your life, or even to learn or improve upon a thing.

Yes, a mentor is better when it's someone that agrees to have contact with you so that you can sit and ask questions. However, that may not always be possible. A mentor can also be a public figure that you can watch, listen to any messages or teachings they've done, and read any books they've written. Jesus should be a mentor for all of us! This weekend, choose a mentor, and if possible make it someone that you have or could have a relationship with. Let them know that you value them and see them as a mentor. Over the course of time, as they mentor you, show them how valuable they are to you.

Every Opportunity

This may be hard, but take a deep look at your day-to-day life. Do you make the most of every opportunity or do you just rush through life? This challenge is designed to stretch you, get you out of the box, and make you more aware of the people and situations around you.

I want you to be careful and use wisdom with this challenge. Keep safety in mind, but don't be afraid. Pay attention to the people around you as you go through your day. Look for open doors to share God's love and possibly even help in a situation. Here are some ideas. You could give change, a bottle of water, or prepackaged food to a homeless person while you're out and about. Perhaps you'll come across a person on the side of the road needing help with a flat, or someone who appears sad or stressed and you strike up a conversation with them and offer to pray with them. The two biggest things to keep in mind are to allow the Lord to interrupt your day and allow Him to use you especially if it means stretching you outside of your comfort zone. This is truly living!

Taming Time

You'd be surprised how much you can do in a small amount of time. Choose something that you do on a regular basis fairly quickly and set a stopwatch to see how long it actually takes you. My guess is that it didn't take you as long as you thought it would. Now set that stopwatch the next time you do a leisure activity like watching TV or doing things online. I bet you spent more time than expected. Now imagine how much extra time you'd have if you took a break from that activity. You would be able to accomplish much more in your day. Your challenge is too fast from that leisure activity and do something that God has called you to do or that you've been putting off. When you're at a loss on what to do, or you are frustrated and wanting to do that activity, pray.

Praise Through Storms

Sometimes we get in a rut with things; even with God. Praise isn't just for when you're in church! It's not only for when you're in a group either. I think that often my praise alone and in private with God is even better than at church. There's no program to follow so you can take as long as you like when you're alone. Some people sing, others dance, and some play music. Those are just a few examples, and I know that some people don't think these are elements of praise; but David danced before the Lord, Moses and the sons of Israel sang to God, and Miriam led the women in praise with a timbrel (small tambourine).

This challenge is to get you out of any routines or ruts you may have developed with God to get you into a deeper relationship with Him. Set aside some time in which you can be alone and not pressed for time. Do something that is outside of your norm. Perhaps that would be praising the Lord outdoors, or maybe walking through your house playing an instrument. Maybe you'll even try dancing for Him for the first time. Do something that shows your love and appreciation for all that He has done. Break out of that rut and enjoy your time with God!

Even the
Toughest of Days
Have Bright Spots,

JUST

DO

YOUR BEST

PRUNING

I am the true vine, and my Father is the
vinedresser. Every branch in me that does
not bear fruit he takes away, and every
branch that does bear fruit he prunes,
that it may bear more fruit.

JOHN 15:1-2 ESV

OFTEN TIMES, A SOURCE OF OUR GRIEF OR SADNESS IS
because of something we've lost or perceived as a loss.
When, in fact, and all actuality, we are simply going
through a pruning process. There are things in our
lives that can be dead or unfruitful, and there is no
reason for them to remain.

Seasons of pruning can be painful. Sometimes we
lose or are distanced from friends or loved ones. At
other times, it can be activities, things, or a set of circumstances. Usually, the things lost are not as
essential as we may think, even when it is something
like a job.

Let's look at that. A lost job, however it was lost, can be very stressful and even devastating to some people. From a worldly standpoint, this is understandable. After all, we live in a time where many people work more than one job to make ends meet. Some people even find their identity in their work.

In the majority of pruning scenarios that I've experienced, things always turned out better in the end. There's an old saying that says, "necessity is the mother of invention" (or something like that). I certainly agree as I have seen it over and over again. Jobs can interfere with our true destiny, stunt growth, keep entrepreneurs from starting their businesses, encroach on time with the Lord or family, and even go against our true values. Many people won't move on a thing until they are forced though. When a person loses a job, they are forced to re-evaluate their life and search for a more suitable source of income. Hear me clearly. I'm not telling you to quit your job! Anyone looking to make such a move needs to exercise wisdom, and have a plan before leaving a job.

A job loss can be seen as a door of open opportunity. People have invented things or started businesses as the result of a job loss. Others go on to learn a new trade, change career paths, or go back to school. It's not always such a bad thing to lose a job. It's painful and trying in the moment, but if we allow it to, it can cause us to grow. The same is true spiritually. Sometimes we are holding on to things that are holding us back. Other times we are connected to people or things that God no longer intends for us to be part of or as deep a part of. Have you ever had a friend that you hung out with all of the time, and then life shifted things to the point that you were barely even able to talk to that friend anymore? It wasn't the result of a fight, but rather that your lives took different directions. This is often part of the pruning process as well.

Remember, pruning is not about being painful. It's about producing more growth or fruit. God will often cut things back or completely off so that we can shift our focus to what He wants us to focus on. What is it that the Lord wants you to focus on right now? Are you currently in a season of pruning or coming up to one? Do you have things in your life that need to be scaled down or cut off?

Father God, I thank You for new growth and pruning, even though it can be painful. I know that it is necessary for my growth and helps me to be reliant upon You and to become closer to You. Please show me anything that You may be wanting to prune or adjust. Help me to accept, adapt, and cooperate with the process. In Jesus' mighty name I pray. Amen.

PERSPECTIVES

\EVERY DAY IS GOING TO HAVE THINGS THAT ARE BETTER THAN other things, or some may say, "good and bad." I prefer to say, "better than others." Did you catch that? It's all about perspectives or how you perceive or look at things. It's a conscientious choice that must be made to change one's viewpoint until it becomes a habit.

Many people in society, possibly even the majority, see the negative in things or find it difficult or impossible to see the positive. Some see the positive, but then quickly counter it with the negative as if there's something wrong with focusing on the positive. It's a glass half full or half empty kind of scenario. There's good and bad in pretty much everything.

> And we know that all things work together
> for good to them that love God, to them who
> are called according to His purpose.

ROMANS 8:28 KJV

Are you one of those rare people that can see good in every situation? A tragedy happens, but then you are able to see how God is using it for someone's good. That's a godly perspective. The problem is we tend to have a fleshly way of looking at things. We think that we're supposed to have an easy life or that things working for our good means no trials or tribulations, that we will live comfortably, get that job we want, win the lottery or something else of the like. When in fact, it's nothing like that. Now that's not to say that God can't or won't do these things for you, but it is missing the deeper meaning and purpose.

I've got news for you. You will have trials and tribulations. Guess what, it will be good for you! Or, it will be good for someone around you. You know it's not all about you, right? Some of you may be confused or angry now, so let me explain.

What God means as working things for our good is not about our worldly good. "Good" is in relation to the spiritual. This means that when we go through a trying time that the Lord is using it to teach us, mold us, shape us, conform us to His image, and to move us towards our next level spiritually. That's a godly perspective and is why some people can find something positive in any situation.

Whenever we are focusing on God and a problem surfaces, the enemy wants us to shift our focus. The problem or issue will begin to grow larger or more intense. At this point, we may become double-minded, and make our problem the same size as God in our minds. That takes us quickly into a wrong perspective in which we are focusing on the problem or issue and not on God. We've then made the issue larger in our sight. Our ability to see God has diminished. We make the problem bigger than God in our minds. This can lead to things like depression, physical ailments, wrong attitudes, and treating others poorly.

Here's a good visual for you.

PROPER FOCUS

SHIFTING FOCUS/ DOUBLE-MINDED

WRONG FOCUS

RAIN: depression, wrong attitudes, treating others poorly

LIGHTNING: physical ailments

God is bigger than any of your problems! It's a matter of staying focused on Him and His kingdom. When we focus on our problems, we make them bigger than God and in effect block Him. We are unable to see God's hand at work in the situation because we are too busy focusing on the negative to be able to look for the positive.

> But seek ye first the Kingdom of God,
> and his righteousness;
> and all these things shall be added unto you.

MATTHEW 6:33 KJV

What's your perspective? Where's your focus?

Father God, I come humbly before You asking that You clean my lens, shift my focus, and help me to serve You, but I need Your help. You alone are holy, mighty, and all powerful. Help me, Jesus! Help me to see every struggle as an opportunity to become more like You and to grow. I ask this in the matchless name of Jesus. Amen.

COUNTENANCE

When Moses came down from Mount Sinai
with the two tablets of the Testimony in his
hands, he was not aware that his face was
radiant because he had spoken with the Lord.

EXODUS 34:29 NIV

HOW AWESOME IS THAT? MOSES' FACE WAS BRIGHT AND
glowing because he had spent time with the Lord!
Have you ever experienced that? Have you ever spent
time in prayer, praise, worship, or the Bible, and felt
great joy and peace wash over you, resulting in a
smile and glow on your face?

Some people are more prone to turn to God in a
crisis, while others forget about Him amidst their
troubles. Which person are you? We shouldn't only
come to God with our struggles. He isn't our personal
vending machine, but we are supposed to take all of
our struggles and cares to Him.

Sometimes on the toughest of days, our only bright
spot is the time we spend with the Lord. We really

shouldn't need another bright spot. After all, He is our refuge
and strength.

> He who dwells in the shelter of the Most High
> will rest in the shadow of the Almighty.
> I will say of the Lord, "He is my refuge
> and my fortress, my God in whom I trust."

PSALM 91:1-2 NIV

> But those who hope in the LORD will renew their
> strength. They will soar on wings like eagles; they will
> run and not grow weary, they will walk and not be faint.

ISAIAH 40:31 NIV

I understand that life can be extremely hard and there are
times we go through some pretty horrible things. However,
we can't go around for days, weeks, months, or even years
on end wearing it on our face. It drags us down and becomes
a perpetual cycle.

There has to be something positive in your life. Let me help
you. The God of the universe handcrafted you specifically for
your life. He loves you so much that He suffered a brutal and
horrific death for you before you even contemplated having
anything to do with Him. You are the greatest of all time.
There can never be another you. Nobody can fulfill the purposes that God has placed inside of you. That's great news
and another bright spot! You are still alive, breathing, and
reading this book, so that means you are still full of purpose!

When you spend time with the Lord, He will reveal His thoughts towards you.

> For I know the plans I have for you,"
> declares the LORD, "plans to prosper you and not
> to harm you, plans to give you hope and a future.

JEREMIAH 29:11 NIV

It is never God's intention to harm you. What can feel like the end of the world, is intended to grow you or prepare you for something ahead or ministry. Sometimes when you experience hard times, it's so that you can truly appreciate the good times.

I strongly encourage you to go deeper in your relationship with the Lord. Spend more time with Him today and every day. When you are in a struggle, spend even more time with Him. Allow God to make your face radiant. Let Him into your situations and every area of your life. Welcome His guidance, peace, joy, and love.

Heavenly Father, I love You, and I come seeking a deeper relationship with You. Please allow me to see and acknowledge Your guidance, to receive Your peace, and experience Your joy and love. I ask that You make Your presence known to me in a new and stronger way. Allow my face to become radiant and let others see You in me. In Jesus' name, I pray. Amen.

FOCUS ON CHRIST

"No one can serve two masters, for either he
will hate the one and love the other, or he will
be devoted to the one and despise the other.
You cannot serve God and money."

MATTHEW 6:24 ESV

HOW OFTEN DOES MONEY FACTOR INTO YOUR TOUGHEST OF days? As adults, we tend to carry many burdens. We may have children, a spouse, or elderly parents that we care or provide for. Some of us are only taking care of ourselves and find that difficult enough. There is a heavy weight placed on money and having enough of it in our current society. The funny thing is that the more you get, it often seems, the more you need. It creates a vicious cycle as we are so concerned about providing for ourselves and our loved ones. Are we trying to serve two masters?

What we so often fail to realize or remember is that we too are children. Our Father is the Most High God! He is the creator of all and has access to all we need.

He provides for all of our needs! Sometimes when we think we need something we don't, but He knows the difference.

Keep your life free from the love of money,
and be content with what you have, for he has said,
"I will never leave you nor forsake you."
So we can confidently say, "The Lord is my helper;
I will not fear; what can man do to me?"

HEBREWS 13:5-6 ESV

Sometimes we create our own problems because we love money or the things it can buy. We may chase after money and end up risking or losing other things just to get it. On the other hand, we may want something money can buy so badly that we overspend and mismanage our money. This can lead to spending money that could have been used to pay bills, or it can lead to debt.

He is telling us that we have no need to worry. God will provide for us. Keep in mind that He will allow us to suffer the consequences of our actions though! It's important to evaluate the situation and see any part we may have played in creating it. Ask for forgiveness and truly repent, if some of it is the result of something you've done or not done. Ask for His help and guidance. God will provide and turn it around when you turn your focus to Christ and His will.

If then you have been raised with Christ,
seek the things that are above, where Christ is,
seated at the right hand of God. Set your minds on
things that are above, not on things that are on earth.

COLOSSIANS 3:1-2 ESV

So, don't try to serve two masters. On your rough days, turn to the Lord and ask Him if there's anything you need to be working on. Trust God, and know that He will always be your bright spot. Focus on Christ, what He has done for you, what He is doing and will do, and heaven. After all, what can man do to you? Nothing! Nobody can steal your salvation and keep you from getting to heaven. Your salvation is in Christ Jesus, not any human being.

Finally, brothers, whatever is true,
whatever is honorable, whatever is just,
whatever is pure, whatever is lovely, whatever is
commendable, if there is any excellence, if there is
anything worthy of praise, think about these things.

PHILIPPIANS 4:8 ESV

Father God, I come bowed humbly before you. Please help me to focus on Christ and the things of Philippians 4:8. Help me to focus on You as my constant bright spot. Deliver me from temptations and plots of the enemy. Help me to remember to always turn to You, but especially in times of doubt, fear, and darkness. Make Your presence known to me and wash over me with Your peace that passes understanding. In Jesus' name. Amen.

SUBMIT

Submit yourselves therefore to God.
Resist the devil, and He will flee from you.

JAMES 4:7 KJV

WE MUST SUBMIT OURSELVES TO GOD'S WILL FOR OUR LIFE.
Sometimes our struggles are because we are resisting
His will or His process of making us into His image.
We need to remember that we are to be kind of like a
lit mirror; being His reflection and light in the dark-
ness of this world.

When our minds are focused on Christ and yielded
to His will, we will naturally resist the devil's attacks.
We long for what God wants, and the devil flees
because we resist him by pressing towards what the
Lord wants. However, when our minds are focused
on our situations, we are ripe for the enemy's attacks.

Be self-controlled and alert. Your enemy
the devil prowls around like a roaring lion
looking for someone to devour. Resist him,
standing firm in the faith, because you know

that your brothers throughout the world are undergoing
the same kind of sufferings.

1 PETER 5:8-9 NIV

We must remain alert to handle the enemy's attacks. It is helpful to know where he usually attacks you and what your
weaknesses are. Weaknesses are areas in which you are more
likely to sin, than in other areas of your life. These are different
from person to person. Some examples of this could be curs-
ing, becoming short tempered, lying, turning to drugs, food,
or alcohol, stealing, and sexual sins. Typically, Satan will attack
you during situations in which you are vulnerable and sensitive; again, these vary. They can be situations related to your
family, fitness, health, finances, and emotions just to list a few.

The enemy's number one goal is to get you off track and
divert your attention. He does this by hitting you where it really
hurts, and usually in a way and time that you least expect it.
When you aren't alert and pick up on an attack quickly, your
focus turns from God and towards the matter at hand. That
then makes the devil and his assault larger than God in your
eyes and can possibly effect those that you influence.

Yes, we have to do our best. Christianity is not about
checking your brain at the door or not having to do anything.
It's about leaning on God and not our own understanding;
allowing the Holy Spirit to lead us. The issues in our daily
lives do need to be addressed in the natural. However, doing
our best in the natural pales in comparison to coupling it with
doing our best in the spiritual.

How do we do our best in the spiritual? Start with praise. We are to praise Him in all circumstances. Even if you can't think of anything to be thankful for at the moment, you can thank Him for being who He is and for your salvation and eternity with Him. Pray. We are commanded to pray without ceasing. Tough days are one reason why we are commanded to do this. Keep your focus on God and all He has done. Then rest assured that He will bring you through this.

So humble yourselves under the mighty power of God, and at the right time he will lift you up in honor. Give all your worries and cares to God, for he cares about you.

1 PETER 5:6-7 NLT

Most Heavenly Father, I thank You for who You are and what You've done for me. Thank You for my eternal promise in You through the precious blood of Your Son. I come to You humbly and longing, longing to serve and please You, and longing for more of You. Help me to maintain a proper focus, and submit to You. Increase my faith and strength. In Jesus' name, amen.

WEEKEND CHALLENGE

Cut It Off

Are you bearing fruit? Keep in mind that the purpose of pruning is for growth and more fruit. In what areas could you see more growth? Do you have things in your life that are stagnant or dead?

Think of yourself as a withering plant that needs strengthening, and God is the Master Gardener. He prunes and provides His water and light to strengthen and grow you. Ponder that for a moment, and think about anything that might be keeping you from receiving what the Master Gardener has in store for you.

Sometimes it is difficult to see things that are right in front of our noses. We need to learn to shift our focus as necessary. This weekend I want you to focus on your walk with the Lord. Take note of anything that's hindering your growth. This could range from something dead in your life that needs cut off, something that's unnecessarily eating up your time and keeping you from spending time with Him, to resisting change and growth because you want your own way. Today, purpose to take action and spend more time with God.

God's Hand

When it comes to perspectives there are a couple of things we want. First, we strive to see things through the eyes of Christ so we can live right and serve better. Secondly, we want to see God's presence in our lives as well as the lives of others.

For the Weekend Challenge, let's focus on seeing the Lord's presence in our own lives. One of my favorite assignments to give to a new student or mentee is to have them write down all the major times in their life that they have seen God at work in their lives. That's what I want you to do. Think of all the major, or even minor events, in your life up until now. Write down the times and ways that you saw God's hand at work in your life. It could be deliverance from a struggle or situation, an instance in which your life was spared, or a time that He provided exactly what you needed right when you needed it. These are just a few examples to help you look. They are in no way a limit of what to look for. Only you and the Lord know all the things He has done for you personally.

Once you've made your list, be sure to go back and re-read it. This is your testimony! Each one is a nugget that you can share with someone to encourage them or draw them to Christ. It also serves to encourage you and increase your faith. It trains you to see God's hand at work in your life and others and helps you to recognize His love for you.

Now some of you may be having a hard time with this. That's OK. Please don't fret. You may need to start small. Start your list with salvation and your life. There you have two, right off the bat, to get you started. The things you see at first might seem small, but at the time they were large to you. Otherwise, they wouldn't have stuck out. Continue working on this list, and allowing the Holy Spirit to open your spiritual eyes. Go back to your list and re-read it whenever you need encouragement or an increase in your faith.

Radiate

Let's radiate Christ's love, joy, peace, and hope in our lives. Do you remember singing the song, *This Little Light of Mine*? Well, it goes on to say that you won't hide it and you'll let it shine. That's your challenge for this weekend. Allow Jesus to shine through you. Go beyond yourself and your comfort zone to share Jesus with others.

Of course, in order to do that, you really have to know Him. To do that you need to spend time with Him. So, your real challenge this weekend is to double your time with the Lord (or even more). Don't let me keep you! I know you're busy. Go! Start now!

Focus Your Focus

It is said that, "Hindsight is always 20/20," but that saying is usually used in a negative way. We say this as a response to when we feel like we (or others that have come to us) have missed the mark in a given situation. We sit and mull over the things that we should have said or done.

Let's turn it around for a positive and have 20/20 hindsight vision for the positive. In the God's Hand Challenge, you made a list of all the times you saw the hand of God at work in your life. These are definitely positive, and a good thing to look back and reflect upon.

Just as we are instructed to focus on the positive in Philippians 4:8, I want you to spend the weekend focusing on the positives in your life. You may need to start with your God's Hand Challenge list to get a jump start, and that's perfectly fine. Create a list of all the positive things in your life. If you say that's impossible because you have too many, just write the highlights and praise God! Once you've got the hang of seeing positives in your life I dare you to take it a step further and find something positive in a negative situation you are currently going through, or have gone through recently. Allow God to shift your perspective.

Direction of Your Run

What direction are you running? Is it towards or away from God? If you are currently running away from God, I encourage you to just stop right now, wherever you are and lay it all down. When you're tired of running, you can rest in His arms. He's right beside you, always was. Since God is omnipresent, it is impossible to outrun or get away from Him. It's also impossible to outwit Him. He simply waits for you to come back to Him for help, peace, and joy.

Perhaps you think you've messed up too bad this time. Well, let me tell you something else. You can't outrun God's love either! No sin is too great that He can't forgive, and the

Lord rejoices over the backslidden that return. Just think of the 99 sheep and the one sheep in Matthew 18. You can go ahead and read it now if you'd like. I can wait. The shepherd goes out to retrieve the one sheep out of the 100. Jesus is the Good Shepherd, and He wants you back.

Maybe you've strayed because you've gotten bored with God. Let Him stir up something fresh in you, and remind you what it really means to be a Christian. Allow Christ to truly lead you in this life and not only will you reap a reward in Heaven, but you'll also live a more exciting and flavorful life here on earth. When you truly follow Christ, you won't have the opportunity to be bored!

I strongly encourage you to evaluate your life. Are you backslidden? The prayer of salvation is at the end of this book. You can go back and rededicate your life to Christ. Give Him your all, and allow Him to use you, mold you, and guide you.

YOUR

NEXT

INTERVIEW

*Will Result
in a Job*

INTERVIEW
WITH GOD

WHEN I FIRST READ THIS FORTUNE, MY MIND WENT IMMEDI-
ately to an interview with God. Since we are all created
for and with a purpose, it would stand to reason that,
of course, He would give us a job. In fact, we have
many, but only some will be covered in this book.

Of course, one has to apply to get an interview.
Usually, when a person wants a particular job, they
also thoroughly check out the employer. The person
will learn all they can about the benefits and requirements. Often times, there will be more than one
interview, and there are interviews as you move up in
the company as well. All of this in the natural can be
applied to the spiritual as well.

Consider your application submitted the moment
you accepted Christ as your Lord and Savior. The
Bible is how you check out your employer, the job
benefits, and requirements. You get to see how other
people have fared in similar positions. You could view

the interview process as how you and God communicate with one another. No matter what, you've already got the job though! When Jesus shed His blood on the cross, it automatically made you a potential candidate for the job.

I'm not going to go over any benefits here because chances are you already know a lot of them. The benefits seem to be taught and understood more than the responsibilities of the job. Besides, you know how to research them for yourself.

Not with eyeservice, as menpleasers;
but as the servants of Christ, doing the will of God
from the heart; With good will doing service,
as to the Lord, and not to men:

EPHESIANS 6:6-7 KJV

Whatever you do, work at it with all your heart,
as working for the Lord, not for men, since you know
that you will receive an inheritance from the Lord
as a reward. It is the Lord Christ you are serving.

COLOSSIANS 3:23-24 NIV

Therefore, whether you eat or drink,
or whatever you do, do everything for God's glory.

1 CORINTHIANS 10:31 HCSB

Notice that God has repeated over and over in His Word that when we are doing something we are to give our all, do our best, and do it as if we are doing it for the Lord Himself. Of course, as with any parent talking to their child, when something is repeated it's because it's important. The parent wants to get the child's attention. Does He have yours? Do you want to work for the Lord? His benefits are out of this world, but that shouldn't be the only reason you want to work for Him. It should be because you love Him.

Heavenly Father, I love You and desire to honor and please You. Please help me to serve You better and truly live for You that others may come to know You and that Your name will be glorified in all the earth. Guide me clearly and help me to know the things that You desire of and for me from day to day. I thank You, and I praise You in Jesus' name. Amen.

DIVINE PURPOSE

WHEN GOD CREATED MAN (MALE AND FEMALE) IN HIS IMAGE, He gave them five clear instructions or jobs.

> And God blessed them, and God said
> unto them, Be fruitful, and multiply,
> and replenish the earth, and subdue it:
> and have dominion over the fish of the sea,
> and over the fowl of the air, and over every
> living thing that moveth upon the earth.
>
> **GENESIS 1:28 KJV**

This isn't just a command. It's a blessing, honor, and privilege that He reserved for mankind alone! No other living creature on earth has so much power, authority, and ability, and I think a lot of people don't realize this.

We are to fill the world with God's characteristics such as love, mercy, and compassion. All things are to be done to His glory, honor, and praise. We are to subdue and have dominion over the earth, meaning that we conquer the problems of this world instead of letting them conquer us. More specifically, God has told us that we have power over the enemy and his henchmen and we are expected to stand against them!

> But you belong to God, my dear children.
> You have already won a victory over those people,
> because the Spirit who lives in you is greater
> than the spirit that lives in the world.

1 JOHN 4:4 NLT

> For we wrestle not against flesh and blood,
> but against principalities, against powers,
> against the rulers of the darkness of this world,
> against spiritual wickedness in high places.

EPHESIANS 6:12 KJV

To multiply and replenish the earth means more than one thing. Yes, we multiply and replenish the earth by having children. Look at the spiritual aspect of it, and we are to be bringing people to Christ and creating disciples.

I do believe that we need to be responsible with our resources as well. Another example of replenishing the earth is to make sure that people and animals are procreating, as well as planting trees and crops. I'm not an extremist or environmentalist, but I do believe that when we tear down trees to build roadways or buildings, we should also be planting trees nearby to replace them. Not only that, but we should get as much use as possible out of the trees that are chopped down.

Having dominion over the earth means that we have the power to rule our world. We have supreme authority from God Himself because we are His representatives or ambassadors on the earth. Satan may currently be the god of this world, but it is ultimately still God's world, and Christ will eventually, in due time, come back to reclaim it all. We will each be held accountable for our piece in the puzzle and whether we fulfilled our assignments or not.

Father God, I thank You, and I praise You for the blessing, honor, joy, and privilege of being Your representative on Earth. I ask that You strengthen and grow me that I may become a better representation of You while I am here. I ask this in the mighty name of Jesus. Amen.

YOUR CALLING

WHEN YOU ARE TRULY SEEKING AFTER GOD'S WILL FOR YOUR life He will have an assignment or job for you to do! Even before you began seeking Him and His will, you probably found that He had you planted right where He wanted you all along. Just because you are now seeking doesn't necessarily mean that He will move you.

> Yes, each of you should remain as you were
> when God called you. Are you a slave?
> Don't let that worry you-but if you get a chance
> to be free, take it. And remember, if you were
> a slave when the Lord called you, you are now
> free in the Lord. And if you were free when the
> Lord called you, you are now a slave of Christ.
> God paid a high price for you,
> so don't be enslaved by the world.

1CORINTHIANS 7:20-23 NLT

Jesus' saving work on the cross has made us free from sin. Paul was talking to slaves here and let them know that just because they had become Christians didn't mean that they should be expecting some crazy life or status change. The same holds true for us today. That's not to say God can't or won't do it, but it is up to Him and His plan and not ours.

New believers may feel like they're slaves to their jobs and think that since they've become a Christian that God will instantly move them out of their jobs. In fact, the chances are that God is going to use them right where they are. The freedom that Paul was writing about was our freedom from sin. He was also adamant about people not allowing themselves to become slaves of this world again because they were slaves of Christ.

> So my dear brothers and sisters, work hard to prove that you really are among those God has called and chosen. Do these things, and you will never fall away. Then God will give you a grand entrance into the eternal Kingdom of our Lord and Savior Jesus Christ.
>
> **2 PETER 1:10-11 NLT**

This goes back to the heart condition. When a person truly accepts Jesus as their Lord and Savior, they allow Him to become Lord of their life. They become new because of Him, and they allow Him to change and shape them into His likeness. By allowing God to have His perfect way and work in you and always growing in Him, you can count on a grand entrance into eternity!

Daddy God, I thank You for all that You have done for me and continue to do. I ask that You strengthen, purify, and refine me according to Your perfect will, not mine. Have Your way in me and through me. Have Your way, Lord! Have Your way! In Jesus' name, amen.

FOLLOWING

WHO OR WHAT ARE YOU FOLLOWING? WHERE DO YOU SPEND your time and money? Are your priorities in order? Let me give you a little hint, if you spend more money on your cable or internet bill than you give to your local church, you aren't following the right things. That doesn't mean just lower your cable bill! It means start giving, start following Christ, start standing for something!

> Then Jesus told his disciples, "If anyone
> would come after me, let him deny himself
> and take up his cross and follow me.

MATTHEW 16:24 ESV

We need to remember that there is a cost for our salvation. A great cost paid by Christ and an extremely minor price paid by us. Don't get it twisted; this is not to say you can buy or earn salvation, but rather that if you are truly saved, you will love the Lord so much that you'll allow Him to rule your heart and life. You'll love Him so much that you'll want to follow Him and you'll desire more and more of Him.

> For with the heart one believes and is justified,
> and with the mouth one confesses and is saved.

ROMANS 10:10 ESV

Again, it comes back to the heart. Such a major part of our salvation and Christian walk, in general, is about the condition of our heart. We have to be careful and guard our hearts, and be careful not to follow chic, catchy worldly phrases such as, "Follow your heart."

> The heart is deceitful above all things,
> and desperately wicked: who can know it?

JEREMIAH 17:9 KJV

It's the Lord that knows our hearts. He knows their condition, secret agendas, hidden intentions, purity, and the like. He will judge accordingly. Knowing all of this, why would anyone want to follow anyone else?

> Every tree that bringeth not forth good fruit is hewn
> down, and cast into the fire. Wherefore by their fruits
> ye shall know them. Not every one that saith unto me,
> Lord, Lord, shall enter into the kingdom of heaven;
> but he that doeth the will of my Father which is in heaven.

MATTHEW 7:19-21 KJV

Jesus was letting people know that their words and actions reveal what is in their hearts. He made it pretty clear that He would be judging hearts. Look at how you are living your life right now. Do you have good fruit? What's your heart condition? Are you following Christ right now?

> But be doers of the word, and not hearers only, deceiving yourselves.
>
> **JAMES 1:22 ESV**

> Be ye followers of me, even as I also am of Christ.
>
> **1 CORINTHIANS 11:1 KJV**

God will put people in your life for a season that are good, godly examples. It is good to follow their example and learn as much from them as possible. In following though, you must be careful not to let them take or put them in God's position. In the end, you must be following Christ above all else!

Father God, You, are who I want to follow and to guide me. Please help me to know when you are guiding me and when I'm allowing my flesh to guide me. Allow me and help me to stay in right standing with You and to continue following You. In Jesus' name, I pray, amen.

TRANSFORMATION

ONE OF OUR JOBS, WHEN WE BECOME A BORN-AGAIN CHRIS-tian, is to allow the Holy Spirit to transform us. We aren't supposed to remain the same! It is an ongoing process until the day Jesus returns or our life on this earth is over.

Therefore if any man be in Christ,
he is a new creature: old things are passed
away; behold, all things are become new.

2 CORINTHIANS 5:17 KJV

But—"When God our savior revealed his
kindness and love, he saved us,
not because of the righteous things
we had done, but because of his mercy.
He washed away our sins, giving us
a new birth and new life through the Holy Spirit.

TITUS 3:4-5 NLT

Our sins are gone, washed away. We are no longer a slave to sin, so we have a new identity in Christ. It's similar to a woman getting married. Traditionally, a woman changes her last name to that of her husband, and she is no longer known by her old last name or identified as single. She has begun a new life with her husband and taken on a new name. As a born-again believer, you have done the same. You've begun a new life with Christ, and you are no longer a sinner, but you are saved!

> if indeed you have heard Him and have been taught
> by Him, as the truth is in Jesus: that you put off,
> concerning your former conduct, the old man which
> grows corrupt according to the deceitful lusts,
> and be renewed in the spirit of your mind, and that
> you put on the new man which was created according
> to God, in true righteousness and holiness.

EPHESIANS 4:21-24 NKJV

The process is ongoing, continuous. That's why we are told in Romans 12:2 to not be conformed to this world, but be transformed by the renewing of our mind. Every day we will be confronted with trials and temptations, so it is important to stay close to Christ, praying, and reading His Word daily. That's how we renew our minds.

> Cast away from you all your transgressions,
> whereby ye have transgressed;
> and make you a new heart and a new spirit:
> for why will ye die, O house of Israel?

EZEKIEL 18:31 KJV

We must turn away from our old, sinful, and selfish ways. Allow God to give you a new heart and a new spirit. Allow Him to do His perfect work in you.

> I will give you a new heart and put a new spirit within you; I will take the heart of stone out of your flesh and give you a heart of flesh. I will put My Spirit within you and cause you to walk in My statutes, and you will keep My judgments and do them.

EZEKIEL 36:26-27 NKJV

It is by the power of the Holy Spirit living within us that we can change, grow, and do what He tells us to do. Remember we are supposed to be doers of the Word, not just hearers. We are able to do it, but are we doing it?

In your personal walk with Christ, are you continually growing or have you grown stagnant? It's wise to take personal inventory periodically. We aren't perfect, but we should constantly be improving. Look back prayerfully on the last six months of your life. Be brutally honest with yourself. Are there any areas that are jumping out at you that are still in need of improvement? What areas have you made drastic positive changes in and how have you grown? Are you a doer of the Word?

Father God, cleanse me, purify me, create a right heart in me. Help me to acknowledge and see the areas that I still need to improve in, but also to embrace the progress I've made. *Refine me, mold me, make me into all that You desire and require of me. I thank You for loving me so much to take the time to do these things with me instead of just discarding me. Help me, Lord. I ask this in the precious name of Jesus. Amen.*

WEEKEND CHALLENGE

Apply Yourself

Let's face it, we can all get a bit lazy or automatic with some things in life. Chances are if we truly applied ourselves we'd be closer to our goals and more effective in various aspects of our lives. That includes our Christian walk. A major part of applying ourselves is to be intentional in all that we do.

Spend your weekend doing a life evaluation. What things are you doing in auto-pilot mode? Maybe there are some things that need to go. On the other hand, there might be some things that you need to add. I understand that there are things we must do, and nobody else can do it for us. I'm not referring to those things.

Determine the things in your life that you need to do and not do. Vow to live your life with determination, intention, and on purpose. Purposefully plan your days, but be flexible enough to allow God to change the plan if needed. Write out daily plans, and if you can find the time, make a note of it when God changes your plans.

Fruitful

How fruitful are you? Do you exercise the fruits of the Spirit? **Read Galatians 5:22-25 for a reminder of the nine fruits of the Spirit.** Remember that being fruitful and multiplying is not only referring to having children biologically born to you. Are you actively involved in the Great Commission? **Go back and read Matthew 28:16-20 again for a refresher of the Great Commission.** Do you regularly introduce people to Christ and help them grow in their Christian walk?

Let's look at another area of fruitfulness. When it comes to life's problems, how do you respond? Look at your knee-jerk reactions to adversity in your personal life. Do you feel defeated, get angry or depressed, give up, or take any other negative stance or action? Do you go to God, pray, look for positives and solutions, praise, or take any other positive steps or attitude?

How do you respond to societal issues that bother you? Are you part of the cause, a complainer, or a solution of that problem? Now that you've evaluated these different areas it's time to do something more concrete. Choose a global or local problem that really gets you fired up and take action! I don't care how large or small your action may seem. Do something! You may do something that seems small like starting a petition to change a law or something that seems larger, like donating a day's worth of your time to counsel troubled teens. Whatever the issue is, God has equipped you to be a part of the solution. It doesn't matter how large or small the role you play. Just do your part, and do it well. All of the parts are necessary and dependent on one another. Be fruitful!

Heart Check

What is your heart's condition? Do you live for Christ because you have a deep love and reverence for Him? Have you allowed God to mold and make you and your life?

Grab a paper and pen and get comfortable. Create a list of the things God has delivered you from. Write down the various ways you've changed for the better and how you have grown closer to the Lord. List all the ways (or at least the major ones) God has used you to serve. Keep in mind that serving doesn't always have to be in public or something major. It could be simply buying groceries for a neighbor in need. Once you've made this list, praise God for those things and pray for the future things you'll surely be adding to your list.

Your Follow

Who or what are you following? Are you busy trying to serve two masters, or are you following Christ while following a great example that also follows Christ? It's important to know who you serve and are connected to.

Get to know who you are following on a deeper level this weekend. If you have a mentor, pastor, or another leader whose example you are following, make sure you know where they are in their walk with the Lord. Don't fall into a trap of trying to follow someone that is behind you. Be sure that you are learning and growing. Eagles can't soar if they are hanging out with chickens or turkeys.

Sometimes we get comfortable and don't recognize our own growth. We then become stagnant because we refuse to move. Sometimes relationships, in which we are following someone's lead, are only intended for a season. We can make things worse by holding on to them for too long. That's not to say that you can't have anything to do with that person, but the relationship will shift gears.

Be sure you know the people you are connected to as well as their heart condition and motives. It's important to follow Christ first and to know that anyone you are following on earth is also following Christ. You don't want to be attached to people with impure motives because it can cause you to shift in a direction that you don't want to go. Even if you don't, it can give others the wrong impression of you and your walk with the Lord. It's a matter of integrity as well as your Christian walk.

Constant Change

One thing people are notorious for is a dislike of change. We as Christians are supposed to be constantly changing though. Believers are to grow, mature, and become more Christ-like every day. We are to be an example to believers and unbelievers alike. We're the representatives for God, so we have to be careful in how we live and how we portray Christianity.

When people see Christians fighting amongst themselves, bitter, or depressed, is it really any wonder they don't want to have anything to do with us? Honestly speaking, none of us want to be that way, even those that are. Is your life a good representation of Jesus and how one of His followers should live, behave, and respond? Yes, even our responses to people matter. People you don't even know are watching you. Are you like an aging cheese or wine? Are you constantly improving as you get older?

You Will
Reach the

HIGHEST

POSSIBLE

POINT

in Your
Business or
Profession

YOUR PURPOSE IN CHRIST

Therefore, be imitators of God,
as dearly loved children.

EPHESIANS 5:1 HCSB

For we are His creation, created in Christ Jesus
for good works, which God prepared ahead of
time so that we should walk in them.

EPHESIANS 2:10 HCSB

WHEN YOU ARE TRUE TO CHRIST AND ALL YOU'VE BEEN CRE-
ated to be, you will be in the business or profession
that He created you for. Walking in obedience, you will
reach the highest point possible for you in your calling.
This means that you do your best to imitate Christ in
all you do in all areas of your life. You are created for
good works that He specifically assigned to you!

There are things that all believers are supposed to do,
like loving others, sharing the gospel, and continually

growing in relationship with the Lord. Then there are things that each individual was intentionally created for. Someone with a love of music and an anointed voice was created to sing, but that doesn't mean everyone was created that way or that no one else can sing. It's just that this particular person has the gift of song. One person may be gifted with their hands to repair things while another may be gifted to create beautiful artwork.

It's important to know your passions, abilities, and irritants. Passion drives a person and fills them with excitement and enthusiasm. It is something they enjoy. Irritants can also drive a person but in a different way. Irritants produce things like righteous indignation that will drive a person to work to change the situation or circumstances. Abilities are easier to define and are the things that a person does well.

The reason it's important to know these things is because it's a package deal that helps a person know what they were created to do and what their assignments are. God placed in you the abilities and passions that you have, and He designed you to be irritated by the things that bother you. This combination can aid you in becoming and doing all that He created you for.

Let me give you an example. A person with an inherent ability to teach and loves children, who is frustrated by their local education system, likely has an assignment as a teacher, tutor, or mentor. Grab a piece of paper and something to write with. I'll wait!

Now, on your piece of paper make three columns. Label one column "Abilities," another "Passions," and the last one, "Irritants." List your abilities, passions, and irritants in the appropriate columns. A word of caution, remember that for our purpose in this activity an irritant is something that causes righteous indignation with a societal issue. Don't list something frivolous like having a rock in your shoe.

Look closely at your lists. Do you have a better idea of what you were created to do? Of course, there are other things that factor into your assignment, but this is a great springboard serving as a starting point for you. This is especially true if you didn't already have a clue as to what you were designed for. Pray over your lists this week and ask God for clarity on your assignments and open doors that you are to walk through.

Daddy God, I love You and want to fulfill my purpose on earth. Please put people in my path to encourage me and point me in the right direction. Give me clarity in all that You would have me to do. Show me the doors I need to go through and the direction I should take. I want to do Your will, Your way. Please help me, Lord. I ask this in Jesus' almighty name. Amen.

FAITH IT
'TIL YOU MAKE IT

SOME PEOPLE HAVE A REAL ISSUE WHEN IT COMES TO STEP-
ping out in faith or taking risks. Anyone that has ever
done anything great had to take risks, work towards
the goal, and fight things like doubt and fear. It
required great faith. There's a saying that says, "Fake
it 'til you make it." My saying is this, "Faith it 'til you
make it." There's nothing fake about faith, and you
don't have to worry about maintaining an illusion!

I am sure of this, that He who started
a good work in you will carry it on
to completion until the day of Christ Jesus.

PHILIPPIANS 1:6 HCSB

Faith is the opposite of fear. We overcome our fear
through our faith, and our faith is in Christ Jesus.
He created you for greatness and a purpose. He will
see to it that the work is completed. You must do

your part though! This requires that you work, take risks, and be steadfast.

A final word: Be strong in the Lord and in his mighty power. Put on all of God's armor so that you will be able to stand firm against all strategies of the devil.

EPHESIANS 6:10-11 NLT

Read Ephesians 6:10-20 now. I'm not going anywhere! I'll wait. Using God's armor is how we remain steadfast and fight off the attacks of the enemy. Fear is an attack of the enemy, and most of our battles are in our mind. The enemy places wrong thoughts in us, and it's up to us to combat thinking by applying God's Word, remembering who we are, what we are called to do, and what God has promised. We must fight off fear with faith.

To faith it 'til you make it, you will have to take risks and go outside of your comfort zone. You can't reach the highest possible point of anything by being comfortable or lazy. It requires work and great faith, knowing that God will see you through. He has brought you this far. It's not for you to quit.

Take a lesson from the ants, you lazybones.
Learn from their ways and become wise!
Though they have no prince or governor
or ruler to make them work, they labor
hard all summer, gathering food for the winter.

PROVERBS 6:6-8 NLT

You have to be like an ant. Most of your life you will not have someone giving you directions, commands, and rules to achieve your goals. The Lord may bless you on occasion by placing people in your life to encourage and guide you, but ultimately the responsibility falls on you. You must use your internal strength to draw strength from God, knowing that He will complete those things that He has started in you.

"Faith it 'til you make it" by putting forth the effort. Get out of your comfort zone and take risks. Don't give up, because you don't know around which corner your breakthrough lies. Apply yourself and work diligently. Don't be lazy. This is how you reach what you strive for.

Heavenly Father, I come before You acknowledging that You are mighty and powerful in all of Your ways. I know that Your Word is true; You will never leave me nor forsake me. You will finish the good work You began in me. It is by my faith in You and drawing strength from You that I am going to press toward the mark. Please keep me from being lazy and place godly encouragers in my life. In Jesus' name, I pray, amen.

PERSISTENCE

The godly may trip seven times,
but they will get up again. But one disaster
is enough to overthrow the wicked.

PROVERBS 24:16 NLT

YOU NEED TO BE PERSISTENT WHILE TRYING TO REACH THE
top of anything. Yes, you may stumble and fall, but
you have to get back up again and keep on going.
Failures are a necessity for success. You're going to
make mistakes, and hopefully, you will learn from
them. Don't keep making the same mistakes. Make
new ones! Don't beat yourself up over them. Learn to
get back up quickly, and move on.

Be kindly affectionate to one another with
brotherly love, in honor giving preference to
one another; not lagging in diligence,
fervent in spirit, serving the Lord; rejoicing in
hope, patient in tribulation, continuing

steadfastly in prayer; distributing to the
needs of the saints, given to hospitality.

ROMANS 12:10-13 NKJV

We are to put others first, be diligent and steadfast, prayerful
and patient, serving, hopeful, and hospitable. This is a Christian recipe for success. A lot of people will backbite, lie on,
use, abuse, and step on others to get to the top or achieve
whatever they want in life. People of integrity, on the other
hand, will help others on their way up; often trying to take
others with them.

May you be strengthened with all power,
according to His glorious might, for all endurance
and patience, with joy giving thanks to the Father,
who has enabled you to share
in the saints' inheritance in the light.

COLOSSIANS 1:11-12 HCSB

It is going to take patience and endurance to reach your goals,
but your heavenly Father will enable you and give you the
necessary strength. Will you remember to give Him the glory?
Will you be joyful and thankful through the process?

Blessed is the man who endures temptation;
for when he has been approved,
he will receive the crown of life which
the Lord has promised to those who love Him.

JAMES 1:12 NKJV

PERSISTENCE

There will be temptations along the way. You will be tempted to cut corners, bend your moral standards, and be like everyone else. You'll even want to quit at times, but you need to remember that you will be blessed in the end. Remember to keep things in their proper perspective.

Father God, You alone have all the power and resources that I need to achieve what You have called me to do. I ask that You help me to remember that. Help me to call on and lean on You. May my dependence always be on You. Strengthen me to endure and live a life of integrity. This I pray in the mighty name of Jesus. Amen.

FIGHT THE GOOD FIGHT

My dearly loved brothers,
understand this: everyone must be quick to
hear, slow to speak, and slow to anger.

JAMES 1:19 HCSB

ON YOUR JOURNEY TO BECOME ALL GOD HAS CREATED YOU to be, you will have to listen carefully to the Lord as well as to those around you. That is not to say that you should be obedient to every voice, but rather that you should pay attention. Even when someone says something that you are not to obey, they have given you something of value to use. At the very least that person has revealed to you their thoughts, opinions, and position. Using wisdom and discernment, and asking God, you can make informed decisions about how to handle that person and where they fit into your life.

You never want to fly off the handle with anyone. Keeping your anger in check is necessary for greatness. Yes, you will need to learn not to be easily offended if you haven't already. When someone does offend you, make it a point to be quick to forgive. Don't allow yourself to walk in unforgiveness.

I know it appears that I went out of order, but I really need to spend some time addressing the importance of being slow to speak. Too often people run with their mouths, saying every little thing that is in their heart or what comes to mind without evaluating what they are saying. Sometimes it isn't even about what you say, but how or when you say it. Timing can be everything. You shouldn't choose to have a conversation with your spouse about a conflictive issue right before they go to work! Save it for a time when you can both be calm and relaxed, can focus on the matter at hand, and have plenty of time.

Typically, when a person is tired or not feeling well, they are more likely to say things incorrectly or things they don't necessarily mean. They tend to be too quick to speak. It is best, if at all possible, to avoid speaking all together on these times or to write things down before you speak. By writing these things down, you are forcing your brain to slow down long enough to evaluate what you want to say before you say it. You are forced to look at your words (literally), and God may reveal potential outcomes of what you want to say, or give you better things to say.

I know that this may be hard for some of you to believe, but there will even be times that it is best not to say anything at all! Not every situation deserves an immediate response, and not every situation needs a response at all. Sometimes the best response is silence and will even earn you respect.

The LORD will fight for you; you must be quiet.

EXODUS 14:14 HCSB

There will be times that the Lord will fight your battles as He did for the Israelites, but it will require you to remain silent. Not every complaint, put down, argument, etc. deserves your time, attention, and words. When you keep your mouth closed in the right situations, you are allowing God to protect you, but if you speak and try to take over, He will allow you to do so. Use wisdom and be slow to speak.

Fight the good fight for the true faith.
Hold tightly to the eternal life
to which God has called you,
which you have confessed
so well before many witnesses.

1 TIMOTHY 6:12 NLT

Maintaining an eternal perspective is very important. When you say things that ought not to be said, you taint your witness. People are less likely to open their hearts and accept Christ if their experiences with Christians are full of mean, hateful, or hurtful words. Don't damage your witness! It's not worth it. Strive to maintain your integrity and eternal viewpoint.

Dear Heavenly Father, help me to bite my tongue when necessary. Allow me to be quick to listen and truly hear Your voice in all circumstances. Strengthen me to truly hear a person's heart when they speak, and to seek to understand, rather than seek to be understood. Bridle my tongue that I may not damage my witness. Help me to be slow to speak and slow to anger, but quick to listen. I ask these things in Jesus' name. Amen.

RUN YOUR RACE

Therefore we also, since we are surrounded
by so great a cloud of witnesses, let us lay aside
every weight, and the sin which so easily
ensnares us, and let us run with endurance the
race that is set before us, looking unto Jesus,
the author and finisher of our faith, who for the
joy that was set before Him endured the cross,
despising the shame, and has sat down at the
right hand of the throne of God.

HEBREWS 12:1-2 NKJV

CHRIST ENDURED THE CROSS BECAUSE OF THE JOY HE WOULD
have from the end result. Not only was He looking to
be seated at the right hand of the Father, but He was
looking at all those that would be joining Him in eternity as a result. He values you so much that He
endured the horrific cross looking forward to you
spending eternity with Him. How excellent and loving is that?

Anything that we may have to endure pales in comparison to what Jesus went through for us. These two verses remind us that we will have to go through as well, but also that we need to keep our focus on Jesus. We maintain our focus on Jesus for two key reasons in continuing our race. The first that is mentioned is the prize. Our prize is eternity with God. Secondly, we focus on Christ as our example. Why is the prize mentioned first? There are a couple of reasons to that as well. Prizes or end results are the motivating factor of why a person does something. Notice, that even Jesus as our example, was focused on the end result rather than His current suffering and circumstances. He did what was necessary for the end result.

We must maintain our focus. We can't allow our sins or circumstances to stop us. That's why this portion of scripture tells us to lay aside every weight and sin. The weight is the rough parts of our life that we find difficult to handle. Our sins can also slow us down when we become more concerned with our fleshly desires.

> Hold firmly to the word of life; then,
> on the day of Christ's return,
> I will be proud that I did not run the race
> in vain and that my work was not useless.

PHILIPPIANS 2:16 NLT

When we hold firmly to our faith and what God says, it is so much easier to endure and continue running our race. We know that there is purpose and a wonderfully glorious end result. Reaching the highest possible point in your business or profession on this earth isn't the final prize. Our final prize is eternity.

No longer will there be a curse upon anything.
For the throne of God and of the Lamb will be there,
and his servants will worship him.

REVELATION 22:3 NLT

This scripture is referring to our life in eternity. Our job will be (as it is now) to worship Him. We are His servants.

Father God, I come humbly before You knowing that my sins are a hindrance to all You've called me to be. I know that the weight of this world distracts me and shifts my focus, but I want to live a life of worship. Please help me to cast aside my burdens, turn from my sins, and keep my focus on You. I ask this in Jesus' name, amen.

WEEKEND CHALLENGE

Pursue Your Purpose

Did you do the activity in the devotion, "Your Purpose in Christ?" You should at least have a better idea of some of the things that God has created you for. In the back of this book, there is a list of resources. Much like your list of passions, irritants, and abilities, the resource list should serve as a springboard to get you moving toward your ultimate purpose.

This weekend, pursue your purpose by finding out where you can get plugged in and connected within your community. You may want to connect with one of the resources or search online for an organization that serves your community directly. The Lord may have even given you a vision to start a nonprofit. Write the vision and make it plain. Do your research, and run with it!

Don't Be Lazy

In order to achieve any of your goals and faith it 'til you make it, you have to be active. Don't be a hearer of the Word and not a doer! Don't be lazy! For faith to be real, there has to be action. Faith in this sense is a verb.

What are you currently doing to step out in faith and proceed toward the goals that God has called you to? Have you at least taken that first step? Do you have an action plan?

Your challenge this weekend is to create an action plan if you don't have one already. In writing your plan of action, you may need to rewrite it a time or two, or even more. Write it out in small, manageable steps and put the steps in the order they must be done.

Let's say your goal is to start a business doing a particular thing, but you need to take a course to learn more, and there are several to choose from. Your list may read like this:

1. Pray.
2. Research course options.
3. Pray about those options.
4. Choose which course to take and enroll in it.
5. Register business name.
6. Complete all legal paperwork and requirements.
7. Obtain phone number and website.
8. Print business cards.
9. Start marketing.
10. Open for business.

Now, this may or may not be too simplistic, but you get the idea.

Write your plan. Take step one, and get to work on it. Don't be lazy!

Others First

I know that in our culture putting others first is counter-intuitive, especially when you are trying to reach the top. Perhaps you are serving in corporate America and are trying to reach the next rung on the ladder. Teach those that are up and coming that may take your position. Share your tricks of the trade. Teach them about integrity, service, and Christ! It is important that they understand how and why you do what you do. You can subtly evangelize on your job as they try to be more like you. That's how Jesus did it. How do you think Jesus made disciples?

Christ had people that followed Him because they wanted to learn from Him, be like Him, and they fell in love with Him. We are called to make disciples. It's quite possible that you are called to do it on your job as you share parts of your life with someone you train. Choose a person you can train to be more like you in a godly sense. It could be your child, co-worker, niece or nephew, someone at your church, or a person where you volunteer your time. Reach out to this person and make it a point to pour into them. Don't worry; God will fill you back up!

Slow to Speak

In order to learn to be slow to speak it helps to learn to be quick to listen. When you hear, you may hear a sound and not pay much attention to it. Listening, on the other hand, is intentional and requires work. Listening is intentionally paying attention to what you hear. Don't just hear, but really listen. Try doing one, or both, of these activities this weekend.

Repeat a story: Listen to a short story, Bible passage, or poem that is pre-recorded or available online. While listening to the story close your eyes and try to picture what you are hearing. When the story is over, write down everything you remember from it. Write the points in order and in as much detail as possible. Once you have done that, go back and listen to it again. As you are listening this time, cross off all the details you got right. Also, write down any major details you missed. How did you do? Feel free to do this activity as many times as necessary and even do it with friends. For more of a challenge choose longer material to listen to.

Conversational Listening: In this activity, there are two main goals in being a good listener. First, do not interrupt. Second, retain as much as possible from what you hear. Have a conversation with anyone about any topic you choose. Have a pen and paper handy. Whenever you feel tempted to interrupt the person, bite your tongue (not too hard!), write down what you want to say and what it's in response to.

Maintain your focus. Keep the conversation on track and don't veer off into something else that is unrelated. When speaking to someone in person be sure to make eye contact.

When asking questions, use open-ended questions as much as possible, and be willing to listen to the answer. An open-ended question is a question that doesn't have a simple "yes,""no," or other short two or three word answers.

You aren't supposed to be a parrot but repeat back some key points throughout the conversation. When you do this, add your understanding to it. Here's an example: "You said that you're tired of Joe taking things off your desk and not returning them. I'm sure that must be frustrating." By doing this, the person you are speaking to knows that you care and are listening.

Worship

What do you think of when you think of worship? Your life is your worship, but your worship may also include prayer, dancing, making music, or listening to music. Of course, these are just a few examples, and worship may look totally different for you. Some people may bow down, sit, stand, walk, or even lay prostrate.

Your challenge for this weekend is to set aside a minimum of at least an hour each day to do nothing but worship God. If you already spend an hour in worship each day, increase that time. Stretch yourself as far as possible, and truly enjoy your time with the Lord.

PLAN OF SALVATION

CHANCES ARE, THAT IF YOU ARE READING THIS BOOK, YOU ARE already a born-again believer. However, I don't want anyone to miss out on an opportunity to begin a relationship with Christ or to recommit to that relationship. Whether you are a new believer or not, there are some things you need to understand.

We are all sinners.

> for all have sinned and
> fall short of the glory of God.
>
> **ROMANS 3:23 NKJV**

The penalty for sin is death, but we can have eternal life in Christ Jesus.

> For the wages of sin is death, but the gift of God
> is eternal life in Christ Jesus our Lord.
>
> **ROMANS 6:23 NKJV**

God has always loved you.

> But God demonstrates His own love toward us, in
> that while we were still sinners, Christ died for us.
>
> **ROMANS 5:8 NKJV**

You are saved by grace through faith and not works.

> For by grace you have been saved through faith, and
> not that of yourselves; it is the gift of God, not of works,
> lest anyone should boast.

EPHESIANS 2:8-9 NKJV

Repent and turn to God for refreshing from the Lord.

> Repent therefore and be converted, that your sins may
> be blotted out, so that times of refreshing may come
> from the presence of the Lord.

ACTS 4:19 NKJV

Declare with your mouth, believe in your heart, and you will
be saved.

> that if you confess with your mouth the Lord Jesus
> and believe in your heart that God has raised Him
> from the dead, you will be saved. For with the heart
> one believes unto righteousness, and with
> the mouth confession is made unto salvation.

ROMANS 10:9-10 NKJV

Be a new creation.

> Therefore, if anyone is in Christ,
> he is a new creation; old things have passed away;
> behold, all things have become new.

2 CORINTHIANS 5:17 NKJV

Remember that faith without works is dead.

> For as the body without the spirit is dead,
> so faith without works is dead also.
>
> **JAMES 1:22 NKJV**

Be a doer of the Word.

> But be doers of the word, and not hearers only,
> deceiving yourselves.
>
> **JAMES 1:22 NKJV**

You may say the following prayer as it is written or in your own words. What matters most is that you believe. Believe the words you are saying and truly mean them when you speak them.

Heavenly Father, I come humbly before You asking for Your forgiveness. I know that I am a sinner, and my sins deserve to be punished. Thank You for sending Your Son, Jesus, to die on the cross for my sins and raising Him from the dead so that I may have eternal life with You. I am now trusting Jesus Christ as my Lord and Savior. I am turning from my sins towards You so that I can be a new creation. I submit to Your will and way. Mold me, make me, remove the things that are not of You and fill me with Your Holy Spirit. Thank You for Your forgiveness, making me a new creation, and for the eternal life, I now have. Please help me to submit to the process,

walk daily with You, and be all that You've created me to be.
In Jesus' mighty name I pray. Amen.

Remember, it's not the prayer itself that saves you. It's the condition of your heart; believing that Jesus Christ saves you. Your Christian walk and new life is an ongoing daily process. Nobody is perfect, so when you sin turn back to God quickly, repent, and ask for His forgiveness. Allow Him to make you into all that He has called you to be. Stay in fellowship with Him and other believers.

Congratulations! Today is the first day of your new life with Christ. Be patient with yourself and submit to the process. Make time each day to study and read your Bible and to talk to God. Understand that you are not promised an easy life, but be ready to have your mind blown. You are now embarking on the adventure of a lifetime!

RESOURCES

Employment/Finances

National Labor Relations Board is the United States federal agency that is responsible for the investigation and prosecution of unfair labor practices.

www.nlrb.org

1-866-667-NLRB

The following is a United States government website. The following link provides information on unemployment benefits and other help for the unemployed.

www.usa.gov/unemployment

Money Smart Family is a financial website that provides smart money resources and tips as well as a Surviving Unemployment & Underemployment Fact Sheet.

www.moneysmartfamily.com

Crown Financial Ministries has free online and printable resources related to your finances and budgeting.

www.crown.org

SCORE is a nonprofit that helps small businesses get off the ground, grow and achieve their goals through education and mentorship. They provide free mentoring services, free online tools and templates, and free or inexpensive business workshops and webinars.

www.score.org

Human/Sex Trafficking

Polaris Project provides information, raises awareness, and serves the victims of the multiple types of human trafficking.

www.polarisproject.org

Zoe International is a Christian, international nonprofit providing prevention, rescue, and restoration services.

www.gozoe.org

Oasis USA is connected to Oasis in other countries and began Traffick Free Communities. They provide education, advocacy, and much more in the US and abroad.

www.oasisusa.org

Love 146 provides survivor care, advocacy, research, and education about child trafficking.

www.love146.org

Persecuted Christians

Rescue Christians literally, physically rescues persecuted Christians.

www.rescuechristians.org

Open Doors USA provides Bibles to persecuted Christians, raises awareness, and has a global watch list of the countries where persecution is the greatest and ranks the different countries.

www.opendoorsusa.org

International Christian Concern provides support and relief for persecuted Christians as well as advocacy, and awareness programs.

www.persecution.org

Voice of the Martyrs has a variety of programs to raise awareness, interact with persecuted Christians, and provide supplies to persecuted Christians.

www.persecution.com

Homeless

National Alliance to End Homelessness is an advocacy and education organization to end homelessness in the US.

www.endhomelessness.org

Home Aid America builds and donates shelters to local nonprofits that address homelessness and help people transition into permanent living situations.

www.homeaid.org

Habitat for Humanity advocates for decent, affordable housing for all, and provides various programs to help families in need of a home.

www.habitat.org

Most nonprofit organizations that address homelessness are local. This way they can be more effective. Here's a link to search for local nonprofit organizations in your area.

www.greatnonprofits.org

Suicide Intervention and Prevention

National Suicide Prevention Lifeline provides free, confidential emotional support for those in suicidal or emotional crisis and education regarding suicide and prevention.

www.suicidepreventionlifeline.org

The American Foundation for Suicide Prevention is involved in research, education, and advocacy.

www.afsp.org

The Jason Foundation focuses on the epidemic of youth suicide and provides education and awareness programs.

www.jasonfoundation.com

The Jed Foundation focuses on teens and young adults educating and promoting emotional health and suicide prevention in this age group.

www.jedfoundation.org

Rape/Molestation

RAINN (Rape Abuse & Incest National Network) provides victim services, public education, and consulting services.

www.rainn.org

Promoting Awareness | Victim Empowerment (PAVE) works to shatter the silence and prevent sexual violence through advocacy, education, and survivor support.

www.pavingtheway.net

The National Center on Domestic and Sexual Violence partners with multiple nonprofits and professionals on all levels to train and advocate for the victims of domestic and sexual violence. Their website has a list of many nonprofits that address domestic and sexual violence in different ways for different demographic groups.

www.ncdsv.org

The National Center for Victims of Crime provides advocacy, training, and connections to various resources for victims of all types of crime.

www.victimsofcrime.org

Abortion/Miscarriage

The National Office of Post-Abortion Reconciliation and Healing offers resources for the variety of people that may be affected by abortion such as the mother, father, siblings, and grandparents. They also started Project Rachel to serve those dealing with the loss from abortion.

www.noparh.org

Rachel's Vineyard provides healing retreats, resources, and education about abortion recovery.

www.rachelsvineyard.org

Bethany Christian Services provide counseling and education for many things including all stages of pregnancy (including loss), adoption, and foster care.

www.bethany.org

The Compassionate Friends provide support for those dealing with the loss of a child at any stage in life including miscarriage.

www.compassionatefriends.org

Adoption

Adoption is a Loving Option offers education, educational materials, and adoption support groups.

www.adoptionisalovingoption.org

The National Adoption Foundation assists people by funding adoptions through special grants and loans.

www.fundyouradoption.org

Option Line connects women with pregnancy resource centers nearest them.

www.optionline.org

The Dave Thomas Foundation for Adoption increases adoption awareness, provides education, and awards grants to adoption organizations that connect children with families.

www.davethomasfoundation.org

Domestic Violence

Reach Beyond Domestic Violence provides domestic violence intervention and prevention services.

www.reachma.org

The National Coalition Against Domestic Violence provides advocacy and a variety of programs, including a program that helps victims in need obtain plastic surgery for their injuries from domestic violence.

www.ncadv.org

Domestic Shelters is an online directory of domestic violence programs and shelters in the US and Canada.

www.domesticshelters.org

The National Center on Domestic Violence, Trauma & Mental Health provides advocacy and education on domestic violence, trauma, and mental health.

www.nationalcenterdvtraumamh.org

Runaways

The Polly Klaas Foundation provides advocacy, outreach, education, and a hotline for people to call for help in finding a runaway child.

www.pollyklaas.org

The CUE Center for Missing Persons provides advocacy, education, search services and assistance for families trying to find missing loved ones.

www.ncmissingpersons.org

The National Runaway Safeline provides a 24-hour hotline as well as online crisis services.

www.1800runaway.org

Safe Place is a national youth outreach and prevention program for young people in need of immediate help.

www.nationalsafeplace.org

Pro-life

Euthanasia Prevention Coalition provides education, research, and advocacy to prevent euthanasia and assisted suicide.

www.epcc.ca

Choice is an Illusion works to keep euthanasia and assisted suicide out of your state and out of your life.

www.choiceillusion.org

National Right to Life works to protect the right to life from conception to natural death through research, education, and political action.

www.nrlc.org

Life Issues Institute has many programs educating the public about the variety of life issues addressing the value of life from conception to natural death.

www.lifeissues.org

Law

Christian Legal Society defends the religious liberty of Americans, promotes justice and provides legal aid for the poor, and inspires and equips law students for Christian service.

www.christianlegalsociety.org

Alliance Defending Freedom addresses marriage and family, religious freedom, and sanctity of life issues by funding cases, training attorneys, and advocating successfully for freedom in court.

www.adflegal.org

Liberty Counsel addresses a myriad of legal issues from cloning and abortion, to religious freedom, religion in schools, the sanctity of life, and much more.

www.lc.org

The American Center for Law and Justice utilizes a strategy of advocacy, education, and litigation to address and protect religious freedoms.

www.aclj.org

Mentoring/Tutoring

826 National offers a variety of programs including tutoring, field trips, and workshops.

www.826national.org

The Tutor Chat Live Foundation provides free online tutoring to low-income students in grades 6-12.

www.tutorchatlive.org

Big Brothers Big Sisters of America connects children aged 6-18 with mentors that receive professional support from the organization.

www.bbbs.org

Christian Association of Youth Mentoring assists churches and nonprofits in starting and/or sustaining youth mentoring programs.

www.caym.org

Pro-Family

The American Family Association spurs activism, informs, equips, and activates individuals to strengthen the moral foundation of American culture.

www.afa.net

The Family Research Council provides education, research, and political activism in defense of religious freedoms and traditional marriage among other things.

www.frc.org

Traditional Values works through education, advocacy, political activism, and grassroots efforts to maintain traditional values in America.

www.traditionalvalues.org

The National Organization for Marriage fights to preserve traditional marriage in America by grassroots efforts, education, and political activism.

www.nationformarriage.org

Other

Prison Fellowship offers many programs for children whose parents are incarcerated as well as their families.

www.prisonfellowship.org

Samaritan's Purse provides spiritual and physical aid to hurting people around the world through various programs and humanitarian projects.

www.samaritanspurse.org

The Salvation Army provides a variety of community, Christian based programs based on the needs of the community that it is in.

www.salvationarmy.org

GLAD Mission works to get Christians involved outside the four walls of their churches through educating and connecting people with nonprofit organizations in their communities that will best utilize their spiritual and natural gifts.

www.gladmission.org